UNLIMITED

Partnership

BUILDING INTIMACY & TEAMWORK
INTO YOUR MARRIAGE

PHIL & SUSY DOWNER

DAVID & TERESA FERGUSON

ETERNAL IMPACT PUBLISHING
SIGNAL MOUNTAIN, TENNESSEE

UNLIMITED PARTNERSHIP
Building Intimacy and Teamwork Into Your Marriage

Phil and Susy Downer
David and Teresa Ferguson
Copyright © 1996, 2007 Relationship Press

Published by Eternal Impact Publishing
Signal Mountain, Tennessee 37377

Second Edition

Library of Congress Control Number 2006909660

ISBN 978-0-9742295-4-6

All Scripture quotations, unless otherwise indicated, are taken from the Holy Bible, New International Version ®, Copyright ©1973, 1978, 1984 by International Bible Society. Used by permission of Zondervan Publishing House. The "NIV" and "New International Version" trademarks are registered in the United States Patent and Trademark Office by International Bible Society.

Scripture verses marked "NASB" are taken from the New American Standard Bible. © 1960, 1962, 1963, 1968, 1971, 1972, 1973, 1975, 1977 by The Lockman Foundation. Used by permission.

Printed in China.

07   08   09   10   11   12   /   7   6   5   4   3   2

Eternal Impact Publishing exists
to provide excellence in resources
for the passion of helping people grasp
and fulfill their God-given purpose
of living life to know, adore, enjoy,
and exalt Jesus Christ and reaching
and discipling others to do the same.

Paul Q. Downer, Managing Director
PaulDowner@DNAministries.org

HOW TO USE
THIS BOOK

If you use this resource as a study guide for your relationships, you will learn how to live your life in a way that impacts others for eternity! As we will explore in the pages ahead, it's through relationships with God and others that life is lived to its full potential. As relationships are enriched, marriages, families, churches, communities, and even entire cultures are positively impacted. Suggested uses for this resource include the following:

Enrich your relationship with God through . . .

- **Daily Devotions**—Use one chapter each week as the focus of daily Bible study and prayer.

- **Scripture Memory**—Study, memorize, and meditate on key Scripture verses in the text which have been included in the "highlight" boxes.

- **Topical Bible Study**—Each chapter includes a topical Bible study which focuses on key scriptural truths.

- **Praise/Worship**—Unhurried times of reflection and meditation will be encouraged in each chapter as you pause to consider the wonder of God's love for each of us.

Enrich your relationship with your spouse and others through . . .

- **Individual Study/Couple Sharing**—Both partners are encouraged to work through each chapter on their own and then come together for an uninterrupted time of vulnerable sharing, encouragement, accountability, and prayer.

- **Men's/Women's Groups**—Men or women covering together the content of each chapter and the biblical perspective. Homework could be assigned to be completed with spouses at home. The group then provides week-by-week encouragement, accountability, and prayer.

- **Couples' Classes and Seminars**—Groups of any size either for week-by-week class instruction (with homework) or for seminars, retreats, and conferences.

- **Couples' Groups/Mentoring**—Two-five couples working through each chapter, first as a couple (see individual/couple sharing above) and then coming together for a time of group sharing, encouragement, accountability, and prayer.

ACKNOWLEDGEMENTS

We would like to thank the many people who have invested in our lives spiritually. In our initial stages of faith, these people included Jim and Mary Gail Lyon, Liane Day, Dave and Judi Hill, and Paul Johnson through the ministry of CBMC.

A special thanks is due to our DNA Board: David Deeter, Paul Olschner, and Dale Burklund; our Advisory Board: Bill and Ellen Armstrong, Jim and Carolyn Blankemeyer, Lewis Card, Jr., Jon and Charlotte Faulkner, Mike and Beth Felix, Bill Hammerbeck, Bill and Judy Hardin, Ken Korkow, Gene Latta, Jim and Mary Gail Lyon, Hugh O. Maclellan, Jr., Jim and Linda Underwood, Eddie and Betsy Watkins, and John Zeiser; our Ministry Endorsers: Pat Morley, Ron Blue, Vic Coppola, Bob and Paula Gilbert, Dr. Howard Hendricks, Bill McAvinney, Duane McPheeters, Scott Melby, Don Mitchell, and Dr. W. Gary Phillips; and our Field Staff Directors: Paul Downer, Jeremy Sperring, Andy Read, Roy Abbot, Brian Ascherin, Mike Behar, Ben Blackiston, Mike Dobbins, Brian Doyle, Dan Erickson, Will Fox, Jim Guth, Jim Morud, David Parsons, Bernie Ritterbush, Lee Truax, Chris Van Brocklin, and Eddie Watkins.

We will forever be thankful for how God has used David and Teresa Ferguson in our lives and we recommend their ministry of Intimate Life to you.

Finally and foremost, we thank our Lord Jesus Christ for His grace, and to Him be all the honor and glory. We pray that the pages ahead will encourage you to embrace the Lord and one another in marriage, and that as you experience God's grace, healing, and joy in your relationship, that you will pass it on and disciple others. Matthew 28:19, 20.

Phil and Susy Downer

ACKNOWLEDGEMENTS

God has abundantly blessed us during this writing process. We are grateful for those who support, encourage, and remove our aloneness.

Special thanks to Don McMinn. Don is a gifted writer who has been a faithful member of the team who developed this material. He, along with the entire McMinn family – Mary, Lauren, and Sarah – spent countless hours under significant time constraints, editing and assembling this resource.

We are also so grateful for Barry Metz. He is a gifted student of the Word and talented writer in his own right. Barry has contributed to the biblical content of this resource and played a critical role in its production.

Finally, since our first encounter with Phil and Susy Downer, we have been challenged and blessed by the dedication and vision of their Great Commission passion. Through our relationship with the Downers, we have also come to know and love these faithful servants: Eddie and Betsy Watkins, Bruce and Simone Maginnis, and Rob and Peggy Robbins. Each of these couples gave us great feedback on the concepts included in this book.

It is a true joy to join with DNA Ministries to further the Lord's enriching impact on marriages, families, churches, and communities.

David and Teresa Ferguson

FOREWORD

"If God can change him, God can do anything." Susy had caught a glimmer of hope for our marriage. Divorce had been at the back of her mind since our honeymoon, but she had postponed the decision year after year thinking my anger would eventually get better.

I had come to Christ after attending a CBMC luncheon and a weekend retreat. Christ changed my life! And Susy could tell the difference. She saw the Bible "working" in my life and within a year she had embraced Christ as her Savior as well. God's timing couldn't have been better. But her incredible spiritual encounter did not immediately heal the wounds I had caused. Because I had hurt her so deeply, she had trouble mustering up any feelings for me at all.

Perhaps you can relate to our story. Perhaps you too have a relationship with God but you are still struggling in your marriage.

In the following pages, we want to share biblical principles and personal experiences which will motivate and equip you to develop a fulfilling, intimate marriage.

This book has been co-authored with David and Teresa Ferguson, founding directors of Intimate Life Ministries. The Fergusons have a wonderful gift of presenting powerful biblical truths regarding marriage and family in an easy-to-understand manner.

Susy and I wish we had known these biblical principles of marriage years ago—knowing them would have helped us through the quagmire and twisted wreckage of our journey. In this book, Susy and I will share parts of our journey, and the Fergusons will share the biblical principles which could have helped us avoid so much pain. Over the last several years we have studied, taught, and cried through the principles presented by the Fergusons. In turn, we have been able to share the material with other couples. We hope this book will be used of God to help you experience His abundance in your marriage.

David and Teresa's journey into marriage, like ours, started out pretty rocky. At their training conferences, they vulnerably share how hurts and pains accumulated in their marriage to the point where, seven years into marriage, laying in bed one evening, David anxiously asked Teresa, "Do you still love me?" only to hear, "David I don't feel anything for you. I'm just numb." From this sense of hopelessness and despair, God began a miraculous work of healing, freedom, and restored intimacy to their marriage.

When we first met the Fergusons, Susy and I had a good marriage, but we still had much to learn. The Lord has used many of the principles in this book to deepen our relationship.

This book is for those who want to improve a good marriage and for those whose marriage is in trouble. The truth is, no one has "arrived." Marriage is a journey, and every step brings new challenges.

In this book we will address some of the following vital issues:

1. Becoming "best friends." In marriage, partners share a lot in common—last name, children, and sometimes even a church pew. But that doesn't necessarily mean we're friends. In the Bible, David and Jonathan had a healthy bond of friendship which transcended business, financial, and family pressures. How can we develop the friendship aspect of our marriage?

2. Living vulnerably. After his defeat at Ai, Joshua was willing to cry out to the Lord in pain, defeat, embarrassment, and uncertainty, and do it in front of his team! Why can't we be honest with our spouse and share the deep issues with which we are struggling?

3. Ministry teamwork. Aquilla and Priscilla lived, worked, and ministered together as a team. How can we operate as

a unit in our marriages by complementing one another's gifts, standing in the gap for one another's weaknesses, and multiplying our productivity, effectiveness, and faithfulness?

4. Great sex in marriage! How can the physical relationship with our partner be the fulfilling and rewarding union God meant it to be?

This book is designed to be an interactive training manual! You will be asked to fill in the blanks, pause and discuss certain issues, and share vulnerably with another person. It may seem uncomfortable at first, but remember—time alone cannot erase our problems or pain. Constructive talk can. Each chapter includes a Biblical Perspective, an Experiencing Biblical Truth exercise, and an Intimacy Praxis. These exercises will challenge your marriage to deeper levels of intimacy, whether used in individual study, men's groups, or couples' groups.

Our prayer is that the Lord will bless and prosper His Word in your life and marriage!

Phil & Susy Downer
President and Vice President,
Discipleship Network of America

David & Teresa Ferguson
Directors,
Intimate Life Ministries

TABLE OF CONTENTS

CHAPTER ONE

Intimacy— Antidote For Aloneness

Phil and Susy's Journey

"I feel like I've been defrauded. You're not the man I dated and you're not the man I agreed to marry." Susy's words hit me like a brick. On only the second night of our honeymoon, Susy concluded that she had "made a mistake" in marrying me. During our months of dating, I developed a love for Susy beyond anything I'd ever known, and I did my best to win her love and affection. It's not that I hid who I was, it's just that no one really knew who I was. I probably didn't even know myself. What I did know was that I was "damaged merchandise" marrying a woman who had never been yelled at before. No wonder our first fight made Susy feel shocked, disappointed and alone.

My angry spirit that erupted on our honeymoon was born years earlier on the driveway of the house where I had grown up. It was there that my father introduced me to his new girlfriend and her two snobby children whom, I was told, were soon to become my brother and sister. I loved my mother, so I deeply resented this "intruder" who was invading our home. It hurt me to see mother wounded so badly. She even went on to attempt suicide twice.

What was my reaction to this hurtful experience? Deep inside my young heart, I said to myself, "I'll never hug my dad again, or cry. Ever." I decided that the only way to avoid getting hurt was to keep people and emotion at an arm's length. That was my adaptation of the great American axiom for men—"Big boys don't cry." That day, as a young boy, I made some decisions that would shape my concept of life and relationships—and adversely affect my marriage from day one. That day, as far as my emotions were concerned, I decided to face life alone!

Both Susy and I were raised to be very independent. Her "dogged independence" and my "it's me against the world" approach to life left us feeling very much alone—*despite* being married.

Our relationship had a rough beginning, but now, after 35 years of marriage and six wonderful children, Susy and I are overwhelmed with the joy of being partners, co-laborers, best friends, lovers, and joint heirs in Christ! Through our relationship with Christ, His Word, and one another, the Lord has healed our marriage.

David and Teresa's Reflections

In our teaching of biblical principles of marriage and family, Teresa and I usually take couples all the way back to the story of creation. Here we see God "setting up" the universe, and we read about God's initial thoughts about marriage.

The first principle we see in Genesis, regarding building intimacy and teamwork into our marriage, has to do with the "aloneness" factor.

Buried two-thirds of the way through Genesis 2, God makes a startling declaration—"It is not good for man to be alone."

God's declaration is startling because although Adam had a perfect relationship with God, He still declared that Adam was "alone." Adam's *spiritual* aloneness had been removed through his intimate walk with his Creator, but even with a perfect relationship with God, God declares that something was lacking. Adam was needy. God proceeded to provide for man's aloneness with the creation of Eve, a helpmate suitable for him. Thus the first stated purpose of marriage was to remove aloneness.

But in Genesis 3, Adam and Eve, in a fatal moment and with a single choice, chose sin rather than God and His provision. Needy by creation, now Adam and Eve were fallen by choice. Their fall brought the return of spiritual and interpersonal "aloneness" and they experienced shame, fear, and nakedness. Just as God had provided for man's aloneness, He now provided for his fallenness. He killed an animal and used it as a covering. Provision for their "fallenness" came as blood was shed, typifying the *"Lamb that was slain from the creation of the world"* (Revelation 13:8). In the dawn of creation, Adam and Eve had two problems: aloneness and fallenness. And God lovingly made provision for both.

> *The first stated purpose of marriage was to remove aloneness.*

We, as descendants of Adam, are in a similar position; we are born needful of relationships with God and others, and we are fallen by nature and by choice. From Genesis to Revelation, the Bible speaks of God's "scarlet thread of redemption" which has lovingly made provision for both our aloneness and our fallenness.

God could have addressed our problems from a distance; He could have simply spoken the solution just like He spoke the worlds into existence. But beginning in Genesis 2, God personally entered the Garden to address Adam's needs, and 2,000 years ago, the Word became flesh in the person of Jesus to fulfill the ultimate payment for man's sin and reestablish the possibility of fallen man's intimate relationship with a holy God.

Across the pages of Scripture, why did God choose to become personally involved in solving man's dilemma? Why did Christ spend so much time with His disciples? Why did He commend Mary for choosing to sit at His feet rather than just keeping busy (Luke 10:38-42)? Why, after the resurrection, did Jesus take time to eat dinner with the disciples? As we study the life of Jesus, one truth is obvious—He placed a high priority on relationships! He was concerned with man's aloneness. But God's concern did not stop there.

At the cross, our sins were paid for and forgiveness became available—but why? One critical reason was that mankind could once again have a relationship with God. The death of Christ on the cross was necessary because we were separated from God by our sins, and the cross provided the bridge back to God. Because of the cross, access to God was now open. As recipients of divine grace, believers can boldly approach God's throne.

But the cross not only addressed our fallenness, it also spoke to our aloneness: *"And I no longer live but Christ lives in me"* (Galatians 2:20); He has come to take up His abode in us (John 15:4); He has also placed us into His body, the Church, so that when one hurts, we all hurt, and when one rejoices, we all rejoice (1 Corinthians 12). Before the cross, we were either Jew or Gentile, and there was no basis for closeness or unity between the two groups, no real resources for breaking down such walls of division. But in Christ, we were made one and He is the head over us all. *"For, He, Himself, is our peace, who made both groups into one, and broke down the barrier of the dividing wall, by abolishing in His flesh the enmity . . . so that you are no longer strangers and aliens, but you are fellow citizens with the saints"* (Ephesians 2:14,19).

Yes, God is committed to remove our aloneness, and He does so through relationships—*intimate relationships*. He provided Jesus Christ, through whom our sense of spiritual aloneness can be removed, and He has given us three other divine relationships—marriage, family, and the Church—through which our sense of interpersonal aloneness can be removed.

Experience teaches us that shallow, surface relationships will not remove aloneness. It is possible to be around people all day long and still feel lonely. It is even possible to be married and feel alone. That's why we say that *intimate* relationships are the antidote for aloneness because intimacy involves a deep mutual "knowing" for the purpose of caring involvement.

As we explore God's design for intimacy, we'll discover some potentials (like becoming one in spirit, soul, and body) and some hindrances (like the unhealed hurt that Phil and Susy experienced on their honeymoon and the baggage from childhood that Phil carried into their marriage).

It's time to check your "intimacy" vital signs:

- Do you ever feel disconnected, distant, withdrawn, alone in your marriage (the secular world often calls this incompatibility)?

- Would you describe your relationship with your children as intimate?

- Can you name three friends who know you deeply and with whom you are open and vulnerable?

On the following pages we begin our journey——our pursuit of intimacy!

Biblical Perspective

WHAT IS MAN THAT THOU ART MINDFUL OF HIM?

God declared in Genesis 2:18, *"It is not good for man to be alone."* To experience God's intended abundance in life, marriage, family, and community, this "aloneness" factor must be addressed. How could Adam have a perfect relationship with God and still be alone? Where does "aloneness" come from?

Aloneness is related to how God created us needing relationships with Himself and with others. There is a spiritual and interpersonal dimension to aloneness which can be described in terms of "vertical" and "horizontal." One can have a relationship with God (vertical) and not be spiritually alone but still be "interpersonally" alone (horizontal). It could be said, therefore, that Adam was alone interpersonally, but not alone spiritually. After the fall, however, this changed. After Genesis 3, everyone entered the world both spiritually and interpersonally alone. And this aloneness is resolved through intimate relationships with God and others.

> *How could Adam have a perfect relationship with God and still be alone?*

Study Questions

Reflect on your need for intimate relationships with God and others. In what ways does God make Himself available to you?

What human relationships has He given you through which He might remove your interpersonal aloneness?

_____

_____

_____

Aloneness is always a relational issue. Spiritual aloneness is answered by a relationship with God. In Genesis 3, God sought for Adam, seeking to restore the broken relationship. Throughout the Old Testament, God resided in the tabernacle or temple with His people. In the New Testament, Jesus appeared as Emmanuel, "God With Us." As Jesus' ministry was coming to an end, He promised the disciples in the Upper Room that He would not leave them as "orphans," but would give them another Helper who would be with them and abide with them forever. He promised that even though He was going away, they would not be left alone. The Holy Spirit was given not just to teach and convict of sin, but to be with us, to remove our spiritual aloneness. Jesus reiterated this in the Great Commission, giving us the promise *"I am with you always"* (Matthew 28:20).

> *What is salvation? What is eternal life? It is the intimate knowing, the intimate experiencing of God forever (John 17:3).*

What is salvation? What is eternal life? It is the intimate knowing, the intimate experiencing of God forever (John 17:3). The moment of new birth is our first experience of no longer being alone spiritually. Our spiritual aloneness is additionally addressed by God as the Spirit comforts in difficulty, illumines the Word of God for personal application, and convicts of sin. When we face judgment *("man is destined to die once, and after that to face judgment"* Hebrews 9:27), Jesus will come alongside us as the "advocate"—we will not face judgment alone.

Study Questions

Think back to the time when you made your personal commitment to Christ. Describe in what ways you came to know Him more intimately? In what ways were you less alone?

_____

_____

_____

_____

_____

_____

If you haven't yet made this commitment, seek out your group leader, a pastor, or Christian friend to help you.

The other dimension of aloneness is an interpersonal one. No amount of education, motivation, or good intentions can remove this dimension of aloneness. In families, no amount of activity, tradition, or discipline can remove it. Within the church, no amount of doctrine, programming, or preaching can remove it. In our culture, no amount of activism, social programming, or civic involvement can remove it. Only interpersonal relationships can satisfy man's horizontal neediness and remove this dimension of aloneness. God has made ample provision for this aspect of our neediness by providing marriage, family, and the church.

We are created with a need to have relationships with both God and others. God, in His goodness, has provided for both needs. Therefore, abundant provision has been made for our aloneness.

Study Questions

As you reflect on God's provision of Himself, His Spirit, His Son, and His Word—just for you, that you might never be alone, how are you affected emotionally?

_____

_____

As you reflect on God's provision of your spouse, children, family, and friends—just for you, that your life might be abundantly blessed, how are you affected emotionally?

_____

_____

How might this stirring of gratefulness in your heart prompt your sensitive care and giving toward God and others?

_____

_____

_____

It's the experiencing of biblical truth that leads us into intimacy with God and with others.

Experiencing Biblical Truth

EXPERIENCING BIBLICAL TRUTH— WHY IT'S IMPORTANT

According to British demographer David Barrett, more than 7,600 people leave the church every day in North America and Europe—"converts to other religions or to irreligion." In other words, one would have to plant almost 8 churches of 1,000 or more people every day of the year to offset the number of people walking away from churches already in existence.

Why do people leave churches? William Hendricks, author of *Exit Interviews, Revealing Stories of Why People are Leaving the Church*, writes this as the number one reason: people no longer evaluate Christianity on the basis of whether it is true, but how it is true in their own lives. The question today is not whether God exists, but what difference does God make?

Recent studies indicate that 78% of new church attenders are seeking ways to strengthen family relationships, but 73% come to believe the church is not relevant to their lives.

> *What is salvation? What is eternal life? It is the intimate knowing, the intimate experiencing of God forever (John 17:3).*

Relationships and Relevance

Churches who reach people in the 21st century must understand these two terms: relationship and relevance.

People are not merely searching for truth—they're searching for how truth can be applied to their lives. They want to experience biblical truth.

An integral part of the *Intimate Life* message involves a conviction that we must *experience* biblical truth. It's the experiencing of biblical truth that leads us into intimacy with God and with others. As we truly experience biblical truth, we move beyond merely obeying rules and regulations and come to enjoy the blessing of intimate relationships. This proposition, if taken seriously, will challenge many current teaching paradigms. As believers, we'll focus not only on hearing the truth but experiencing it. As Christian leaders and teachers, we'll no longer be satisfied with merely imparting spiritual truth in a relevant manner, but we'll see the necessity of having people experience what they're learning—right in their own marriages, families, and friendships!

Couple or Group Activity: Have each spouse or group member select three of the "one anothers" listed below that they would most like to see more of at home. After sharing and praying together, make it a goal over the next month to consciously live out these "one anothers" in your home and group.

- Love one another (John 13:34).

- Depend on one another (Romans 12:5 AMP).

- Be devoted to one another (Romans 12:10).

- Out-do one another in showing honor (Romans 12:10).

- Rejoice with one another (Romans 12:15, 1 Corinthians 12:26).

- Weep with one another (Romans 12:15).

- Be of the same mind toward one another (Romans 12:16).

- Don't judge one another (Romans 14:13).

- Receive one another (Romans 15:7).

- Admonish one another (Romans 15:14).

- Greet one another (Romans 16:16).

- Wait for one another (1 Corinthians 11:33).

- Care for one another (1 Corinthians 12:25).

- Serve one another (Galatians 5:13).

- Be kind to one another (Ephesians 4:32).

- Forgive one another (Ephesians 4:32, Colossians 3:13).

- Be tenderhearted toward one another (Ephesians 4:42).

- Encourage one another (1 Thessalonians 5:11).

- Submit to one another (Ephesians 5:21).

- Forbear with one another (Ephesians 4:2, Colossians 3:13).

- Stimulate love in one another (Hebrews 10:24).

- Show hospitality to one another (1 Peter 5:5).

- Minister gifts one to another (1 Peter 4:10).

- Be clothed in humility one toward another (1 Peter 5:5).

- Don't speak evil against one another (James 4:11).

- Don't grumble against one another (James 5:9).

- Confess your faults one to another (James 5:16).

- Pray for one another (James 5:16).

- Fellowship with one another (1 John 1:7).

- Don't be puffed up against one another (1 Corinthians 4:6).

- Bear one another's burdens (Galatians 6:2).

Accountability note: Encourage one another unto love and good deeds (Hebrews 10:24) as you check up on each group member.

Praxis

CHILDHOOD QUESTIONNAIRE

It's impossible to be intimate with someone you don't know. A great way to truly "know" another person is to explore together your growing up experiences. This enables friends to develop a much deeper understanding of one another and marriage partners to see additional ways in which they must "leave" their family of origin. Complete the following inventory and then share together with your spouse or group member.

1. If you grew up with both parents in the home, how did you know they loved each other when you were young? How did they show it? (For instance: they hugged and kissed a lot, they spoke kindly to each other, they laughed a lot together.)

   _____

   _____

   _____

2. Indicate **mom**, **dad**, **both**, or **neither** next to the following phrases to help describe your home life as a child.

   Family leader -

   Main disciplinarian -

Quick temper -

Comfortable giving affection to me -

Hard to please -

Parent I felt closest to -

3. How did mom and dad handle conflict with you?

Dad would -

Mom would -

4. Check any of the following phrases that seem to describe remembrances about your childhood:

❑ Our family appeared normal to everyone else—but it wasn't.

❑ I was cared about because of the things I did—my performance.

❑ I was loved for who I was—my character.

❑ I felt like an outsider, an observer of the rest of the family.

❑ Our home was demanding and performance-based with lots of rules.

❑ I often felt alone.

❑ I always felt like we "walked on eggshells" around our house.

❏ I seemed to always be the adult, even when my parents were around.

❏ It was always extremely important for me to please everyone.

5. Now that you're an adult and have observed families, what do you think was possibly missing in yours? (For example, "I realize now my mom was overly controlling. My parents didn't make me feel very secure. We could have used a lot more joy and laughter around my house.")

_____

_____

_____

6. Do you think some of your experiences as a child may be negatively affecting how you relate to your spouse? In what ways? (For instance, "I resist my wife's suggestions because they remind me of my controlling mother." "I need a lot of my husband's attention because I didn't get it from my dad.")

_____

_____

_____

7. How did you feel as you were completing the above questions?

_____

_____

_____

8. When you have finished this exercise, be sure to set aside plenty of time to discuss your responses with your spouse.

Listen carefully and responsively to all that your partner says. Share comforting words, pray together for God's freedom and peace, and then discuss contributions each of you could make toward enriching your marriage.

_____

_____

_____

_____

CHAPTER TWO

Exploring Deeper Intimacy Needs

INTIMACY MEANS MORE THAN SEX

Phil and Susy's Journey

Before I married Phil, I knew he had been with other women, but I was sure of his love for and devotion to me, and I assumed our physical relationship after marriage would be wonderful and fulfilling. However, on the second night of our honeymoon, Phil became irritated and frustrated and then took his anger out on me with a barrage of accusations and criticisms. I had never heard such uncontrollable anger. In fact, I was 21 years old and had never even been yelled at before. And now I was married to a "screamer." I cried myself to sleep that night wondering, "Who is this man I have married?" Certainly not the man I fell in love with.

One of the hardest aspects of dealing with Phil's anger was not only the pain it caused me, but his expectation that after he "blew his stack," the appropriate way to heal the hurt was to be physically intimate. I didn't refuse, but on the inside I was resentful and hurt. From that day forward, I had to live with the uncertainty of not knowing when Phil would turn on me as though I were his enemy.

When we first got married, I really loved Susy with all my heart. I just couldn't get along with her. The truth was, I had a hard time getting along with anyone for very long in any type of close relationship. In Viet Nam, my friend and fellow machine-gunner, Ralph, described me as more dangerous than the North Vietnamese army when I got angry. Growing up, my mother told me that she was never allowed to express emotion, so she encouraged me to express mine—any way I wanted.

Even after Susy and I became Christians, we probably would have divorced had it not been for some caring friends in the Christian community who discipled us. A doctor named Jim met with me for almost three years as we studied the "Operation Timothy" books (a discipleship course produced by CBMC). A woman named Liane also met with Susy for a year using the same study. Then Jim and his wife Mary Gail met with us as a couple every week for three years. Through that time of discipleship, we saw first-hand how Christians deal with relational issues and how we could grow in Christ. Through their faithful example and the teaching of Scripture, we began the long process of analyzing our differences and the pain we had inflicted on each other, and we began to move forward.

During our discipleship time we studied and memorized key Bible passages dealing with marriage such as Ephesians 4:26, 27, and 29, and Ephesians 5:21, 25, and 29. Sometimes our experiences with Scripture were merely intellectual. We had truth in our heads, but it was not affecting our walk. For instance, James 5:16 says, *"Therefore confess your sins to each other and pray for each other so that you may be healed."* Many men have had the honesty to confess to me the bad attitudes, selfish conduct, and hurtful behaviors they have displayed toward their wives. But when I told them that they needed to tell their wives the things they were telling me, they actually looked surprised. There's a difference between intellectually knowing truth and actually experiencing it.

Perhaps the most significant way in which I have learned to experience biblical truth is in the area of intimacy needs. Through our exposure to Intimate Life Ministries we have learned that just as God created us with physical needs such as air, food, and water, He also created us with intimacy needs.

I'll let David and Teresa explain.

David and Teresa's Reflection

In order to rebuild broken relationships and to live together peaceably, we must understand ten commonly identified intimacy needs.

Each of us has unique and special relational needs which when met, produce the experience and "feelings" of being loved. It's important not only to *know* that I'm loved mentally, but also to *experience* it emotionally and behaviorally. The emotional feelings of love are very often, for example, related to needs for attention, affection and appreciation being met. Understanding an individual's significant relational needs helps equip us to better love this person as we play a role in helping meet some of these needs. As a back-drop for better understanding this relationship between love and needs, we first need to review God's love for us.

God Meets Needs!

"God demonstrated his love toward us . . . " (Romans 5:8). It's this demonstration of love that is meaningful. God doesn't simply "verbalize" His love—He demonstrates it. One meaningful way to better understand this demonstration of love is to view God's role in meeting your needs. There's a need for forgiveness which is met in Christ's death. There are needs for acceptance and for renewed purpose which are met in Christ. The needs for cleansing, strength, discernment, and guidance are met through Christ's gift of the Holy Spirit. On and on we could go, but the key realization is this: How do I know and experience God's love for me? He has met and continues to meet my needs!

Whether you realize it or not, two significant truths are at work in your relationships. These truths are either working "for" you or "against" you.

Basic Needs Met = Fulfillment

Every person has basic relational needs which, when met, produce a sense of fulfillment, joy, and strength—especially in marriage. Some of these basic needs are easily identified while others are "discovered" by trial and error. Needing to feel secure in marriage fidelity for example, is an easily identified need. The need to be appreciated for contributions to our family and for character strengths might be less obvious—and thus discovered after a family member "explodes" after feeling unimportant, taken-for-granted, and used. A marriage with an abundance of met needs will retain romance and be better protected from temptations. A family which focuses on giving to meet one another's needs will experience closeness, affirm each other's value, and serve as a powerful example to a self-centered world.

Basic Needs Unmet = Frustration

You have a basic physical need for sleep and when it goes unmet you feel uptight, irritable, and easily frustrated. It's the same with basic relational needs. A marriage partner who goes for long periods without attention, affection, or appreciation can easily become vulnerable to moodiness, retaliation, or rejection. A child who misses out on approval, attention, or comfort might begin to "act out" in order to gain attention or strike out against those who withhold such basic needs.

God created us with these intimacy needs. For instance, we all seem to have the need for: acceptance, affection, appreciation, approval, attention, comfort, encouragement, respect, security, and support. Recognizing these needs is not admitting weakness. It is accepting how God has made us and how we are designed to minister to each other.

These intimacy needs are cross-cultural (Asians, Africans, Anglos—all nationalities have these needs), life-long (needs don't diminish with age or maturity—a senior adult has the same needs as a child), and continuous (needs can never be met "once-for-all," they must constantly be met). God has promised to meet our needs (Philippians 4:19), but He often chooses to do so through other people—us!

Here is a list of ten key intimacy needs and biblical references which encourage our selfless giving to one another:

- **Acceptance**—Deliberate and ready reception with a favorable response; to receive willingly; to regard as good and proper. *"Wherefore accept one another, just as Christ also accepted us to the glory of God"* (Romans 15:7).

- **Affection**—To communicate care and closeness through physical touch and affirming words. *"Greet one another with a holy kiss"* (Romans 16:16).

- **Appreciation**—To recognize with gratitude; to communicate with words and feelings, personal gratefulness for another person; to praise. *"I praise you . . . "* (1 Corinthians 11:2).

- **Approval**—To accept as satisfactory; to give formal or official sanction to; to have or express a favorable opinion; to approve of. *"Because anyone who serves Christ in this way is pleasing to God and approved by men"* (Romans 14:18).

- **Attention**—To take thought of another and convey appropriate interest, concern, and support; to enter into another's world. *"But that the members (of the body) should have the same care for one another"* (1 Corinthians 12:25).

- **Comfort**—To give strength and hope to; to ease grief or trouble; to console, cheer. *"The God of all comfort, who comforts us in all our troubles, so that we can comfort those in any trouble"* (2 Corinthians 1:3,4).

- **Encouragement**—To urge forward and positively persuade toward a goal; to inspire with courage, spirit, or hope; to stimulate. *"Therefore encourage one another and build each other up"* (1 Thessalonians 5:11).

- **Respect**—To value and regard highly; to convey great worth; to esteem. *"Show proper respect to everyone"* (1 Peter 2:17).

- **Security**—Freedom from exposure to danger; to put beyond hazard of losing, want, or deprivation; confidence of "harmony" in relationships. *"May those who love You be secure"* (Psalm 122:6).

- **Support/Bear Burden**—To come alongside and gently help carry a burden; to assist in a struggle or problem; to provide for. *"Carry each other's burdens, and in this way you will fulfill the law of Christ"* (Galatians 6:2).

Pause and reflect on which three needs you might most enjoy receiving from your spouse, and then guess which three your spouse might most enjoy receiving from you. At the end of the chapter we'll work together on these exercises.

Phil and Susy's Journey

As we studied these intimacy needs, we began to understand how different we were. For example, Susy and I both need appreciation, but the specific way we like to receive it is different. Susy feels appreciated when I do something nice or helpful for her; I feel appreciated when she refrains from correcting me in public, and when she expresses her appreciation to me in words. Likewise, we both want to respect each other and to be respected. Susy feels respected when I listen to her advice, even if I don't take it. I feel respected when she takes my advice (when we both agree that it's right).

We both need approval, but because of my insecure background, I need to hear it far more often.

David and Teresa's Reflections

Pause and take a minute to write out an example of what each of these ten needs might "look like" to you in your marriage:

I sense my partner's:

- acceptance when _____
- affection when _____
- appreciation when _____
- approval when _____
- attention when _____
- comfort when _____
- encouragement when _____
- respect when _____
- security when _____
- support when _____

Phil and Susy's Journey

As I was working through the material on "Intimacy Needs," I realized that these needs—met or unmet—greatly influence the sexual aspect of the marriage relationship. When we were first married, I was totally ignorant as to the wonderful way that God had "wired" our wives relative to their physical desire. For a woman, emotional intimacy and physical intimacy are intricately entwined.

Another way that intimacy needs and the physical relationship are related is the whole area of guarding one's heart and mind. It is very difficult, if not impossible, for a man to meet any of the ten intimacy needs of his wife if he is engaging in impure thoughts and activities, because our thought-life is known by the Lord, and sin hinders our fellowship with God and the ones we love. Also our wives intuitively know that things are not right, even if they don't know for sure what we're thinking. Here are some suggestions for how men can protect their minds and hearts in the area of sexual sin. Susy also has corresponding suggestions for women.

Phil's List

1. Scripture is clear that the eye is the gateway to the heart. So many years ago I made a covenant with my eyes like Job did, as he writes in Job 31:1, *"I made a covenant with my eyes not to look lustfully at a girl."* I purposed that I would not look at anything or anyone that would defile, hamper, or discourage my relationship with the Lord or my relationship with my wife. As a result, before I even unpack my suitcase when I stay in hotel rooms alone, I pray over the room and quote Colossians 3:5-9, *"Put to death, therefore, whatever belongs to your earthly nature: sexual immorality, impurity, lust, evil desires and greed, which is idolatry. Because of these, the wrath of God is coming. You used to walk in these ways, in the life you once lived. But now you must rid yourselves of all such things as these: anger, rage, malice, slander, and filthy language from your lips."*

2. One of the reasons many men fall into sexual sin is that they counsel women. It's dangerous for a man to allow a woman to share intimate subjects with him such as problems, hurts, and pains. Women should counsel women. Men should counsel men.

3. I have several accountability groups that I meet with for different areas of my life, and in each one I ask the men to examine my life with respect to my commitment to purity. One of these groups is extremely aggressive. We spend a lot of time questioning each man over every aspect of his life. It's hard to hide from men who get to know you this well and spend so much time sifting through your life.

4. Because I have made this covenant with my eyes and ears, my entire focus and desire is on Susy and no one else. This is God's intention—that we be focused only on our wives. Because of this singular focus, I find increasingly that while Susy may not have the same youthful look she did at twenty years of age and before six children, she is still the most exciting, appealing, attractive, and sexy woman I know.

Susy's List

1. As a woman, I'll never fully understand the visual attraction men have for women. I know that God made men this way so I want to help Phil avoid things that could cause him and our sons, Paul, Matt, and Josh, to stumble. For example, Phil told me that some things that I received in the mail, most of which came unsolicited, were sources of temptation. I finally had to request that they take our name off their mailing lists. I even try to get the underwear catalogues out of the mail before the men of our house stumble onto them.

2. Often Phil mentions deliberate steps that he takes to avoid situations that could be misunderstood or compromising. Instead of not understanding or making light of such discussions, I try to support him by complimenting and

encouraging him for taking such precautions. Many women do not understand the depth of pressure and the pervasiveness of temptation that the world offers to our husbands.

3. I have wonderful sisters in Christ to whom I am accountable and have always wanted Phil to be involved in accountability groups as well. I encourage these times and do not resent the time he's away from the family during these meetings. He always tries to be sensitive and considerate relative to the timing and duration.

4. When we eat at a restaurant, I appreciate the fact that Phil wants me to sit in the chair facing the room and he sits in the chair facing the wall, just so he won't be distracted. This really makes me feel respected, loved, and accepted.

David and Teresa's Reflections

It's time for another quiz:

- How well do you know your spouse's most important needs?
- How do these needs, when they are met or unmet, affect your physical relationship?
- What hindrances often plague your pursuit of intimacy?

The following exercises will help you answer these questions.

Biblical Perspective

INTIMATE RELATIONSHIPS—THEY MUST BE DEVELOPED AND PROTECTED.

Intimacy doesn't just "happen"; it takes conscientious effort to develop close, meaningful relationships. And once intimacy is established, it must be protected. This twofold emphasis is seen in John 10:10, which says, *"The thief comes only to steal and kill and destroy* (Satan wants to destroy the closeness we have with God and others); *I have come that they may have life, and have it to the full"* (one of the ways we experience a meaningful life is through intimacy with God and others).

> *"Get rid of all bitterness, rage and anger . . . . Be kind and compassionate to one another, forgiving each other, just as in Christ God forgave you"* *(Ephesians 4:31,32).*

Intimacy can be developed through:

- Affectionate Caring—"I care about you."

- Vulnerable Communication—"I trust you."

- Joint Accomplishment—"I need you."

- Mutual Giving—"I love you."

Intimacy must be protected from:

- Emotional bondage (hinders affectionate caring)

- Fear (hinders vulnerable communication)

- Self-sufficiency (hinders joint accomplishment)
- Selfishness (hinders mutual giving)

Let's take a closer look at these common hindrances to intimacy.

Affectionate Caring Hindered By Emotional Bondage

It's difficult, if not impossible, to have a caring, loving spirit if you're filled with bitterness, guilt, rage, and anger. And these emotions/sins will damage all of your relationships, not just the ones to which the anger is directed. For instance, if you're angry with your boss, that anger will not only hurt that relationship but also your relationships with your spouse, children, and friends. Anger poisons the soul.

Ephesians 4:31-32 teaches us that we must "get rid of" these vices (turn loose of, put away, empty out). This is done through forgiveness. Past hurts, even those suffered in childhood, must be dealt with properly in order to gain emotional freedom. Then we'll be free to be "kind and compassionate," and be able to engage in affectionate caring.

The guilt I feel over my unChristlike actions can be resolved through proper confession (1 John 1:9, James 5:16).

Study Questions

At times I find myself holding onto anger concerning . . .

_____

_____

At times I sense conviction of my guilt concerning . . .

_____

_____

Vulnerable Communication Hindered by Fear

Various manifestations of fear will hinder vulnerable communication:

- If I fear your criticism or rejection, I'll hold back from sharing my feelings, hurts, or needs.

- If I fear my own inadequacy, I'll hesitate to take initiative and avoid emotionally challenging conversations.

- If I fear being hurt, disappointed, or used, I may seek to control all situations to avoid any vulnerability.

- If I question your sincerity, genuineness, or commitment, I may demand to have it "proven" before I can accept it.

As we begin to understand and experience the perfect love of God, our personal fears are eliminated and we're able to vulnerably relate to God. As we learn to apply His perfect love to human relationships, these relationships mature, trust develops, and vulnerability deepens.

"There is no fear in love, but perfect love drives out fear" (1 John 4:18).

At times I sense anxiety or fear concerning . . .

_____

_____

Joint Accomplishment Hindered by Self-Sufficiency

A "Maverick, Lone Ranger" mentality is damaging to every relationship. If I think I can make it on my own, why do I need you?

The truth is, we need each other! God created us to be mutually giving to each other. Practically speaking, no one person has all the gifts, talents, skills, and resources needed to get the job done.

Self-sufficiency often develops through prolonged periods of unmet needs and the associated hurt which drives a person to deny their needs or to turn to self-nurturing practices to meet them (eating, fantasizing, achievement, perfectionism, and other forms of escape). Self-sufficiency is also reinforced by the "stoic, macho, hero" mentality which is often encouraged in our society.

> *"I am rich; I have acquired wealth and do not need a thing"* (Revelation 3:17).
>
> *"Apart from Me you can do nothing"* (John 15:5).

To the contrary, when we look to one another and say, "I need you; I can't do this without you," or "we did it together!" intimacy deepens.

I am tempted to become self-sufficient and self-reliant when . . .

_____

_____

I handle it by . . .

_____

_____

Mutual Giving Hindered by Selfishness

Unfortunately, we often get so obsessed with our own needs that we neglect giving to the needs of others and we begin to "take" to have our needs met. Many relationships can be characterized by a take/take mentality, but there's no satisfaction in taking to have our needs met (there's a big difference between "taking" a hug and lovingly being "given" one). A relationship characterized by taking will soon show signs of resentment, discouragement, and distance. A relationship characterized by mutual giving will be satisfying, abundant, and intimate.

I find myself selfishly "taking" at times concerning . . .

_____

_____

Take a quick check of your "relational vital signs." Do you have unresolved emotional baggage? Are you hindered by fear? Are you self-sufficient or selfish? To whatever degree these hindrances have crept into your life, they will adversely affect your ability to closely relate to others. Discuss these issues with your spouse or a close friend.

"Do nothing out of selfish ambition or vain conceit, but in humility consider others better than yourselves" (Philippians 2:3).

Experiencing Biblical Truth

TOP 10 INTIMACY NEEDS

L ook over this list of ten intimacy needs. First, mark the three (3) needs you consider the most important for you to receive from your spouse. Next, mark the three (3) needs you think your spouse would consider most important to receive from you.

Myself   *My Spouse*

❑   **Acceptance**—deliberate and ready   ❑
        reception with a favorable, positive
        response (Romans 15:7).

❑   **Affection**—to communicate care and   ❑
        closeness through physical touch and
        affirming words (Romans 16:16).

❑   **Appreciation**—to communicate with   ❑
        words and feelings and personal
        gratefulness for another (1 Corinthians
        11:2).

❑   **Approval**—expressed commendation; to   ❑
        think and speak well of (Romans 14:18).

Myself   My Spouse

❏   **Attention**—to take thought of another   ❏
      and convey appropriate interest and
      support; to enter into another's world
      (1 Corinthians 12:25).

❏   **Comfort** (empathy)—to come alongside   ❏
      with word, feeling and touch; to give
      consolation with tenderness (Romans
      12:15).

❏   **Encouragement**—to urge forward and   ❏
      positively persuade toward a goal (1
      Thessalonians 5:11, Hebrews 10:24).

❏   **Respect**—to value and regard highly;   ❏
      to convey great worth (Romans 12:10).

❏   **Security**—confidence of harmony in   ❏
      relationships; free from harm (Romans
      12:16a).

❏   **Support**—come alongside and gently   ❏
      help carry a load (Galatians 6:2).

First, compare your "top three" with your spouse's "top three." How many are the same (3, 2, 1, 0)? It's not uncommon to have only "1" or "0" the same. This shows how often we're tempted to give our spouse, not what he or she needs, but what we need!

Discuss with your spouse why you chose the three you chose for yourself. In this sharing time, don't criticize your spouse.

How well did you do in selecting your partner's top three?

How could you specifically meet one or two of your partner's top three needs this week?

Praxis

ENHANCING SEXUAL INTIMACY

The writer of Hebrews exhorts us that, *"the marriage bed (should be) kept pure"* (Hebrews 13:4). The best way to preserve the sanctity of the marriage bed is to maintain a vital and satisfying sexual relationship. Here are three suggestions for keeping the "sizzle" in your sex life.

Increased Sexual Desire

Sex is not all in your head, but a great deal of it is! Many couples enhance the "passion" dimension by letting their minds begin to wander over pleasurable thoughts of their spouse; maybe beginning in the morning after a tender and affectionate parting, during an afternoon bubble bath or during a relaxed reading of *Solomon on Sex* (Dillow, 1977).

A balanced relationship will also include touch in three ways:

- **Spiritual Touching**—Holding hands to pray communicates common spiritual agreement. Touch in church, embrace one another at times of great joy, and hold hands as a family at the dinner prayer.

- **Soul Touching**—Embrace one another as you depart and as you re-unite. Go for a walk holding hands, walk arm in arm through the mall, sit close to one another in the car, and "claim" one another through your embrace when you're out in public.

• **Sexual Touching**—Soft skin touching is usually preferred over grabbing or mauling. Kiss "brushing" of neck, back, or hand is often appropriate. Try body massage with lotion or baby oil. Fabrics can accentuate touch so you might try silk sheets or silk nightwear.

Sharing Preferences Through Love Maps

I. Complete your Love Map

From my point of view, a perfect sexually intimate time with my spouse would include the following:

1.

2.

3.

4.

5.

6.

II. Marriage Intimacy

- Exchange your Love Maps—pick a private time and place.

- Discuss them as much as you are comfortable.

- Clarify and answer questions as appropriate.

- Free your spouse to fulfill as much of your Love Map as he or she is comfortable with . . . don't insist, get pushy, or love conditionally!

III. Give to One Another—Scheduling two times of intimacy to fulfill both Love Maps

- Husband should first "give" in fulfilling his wife's Love Map, with a subsequent time for the wife to "give."

- Schedule–plan a time for this so you can both anticipate it.

- Throughout the day, spend moments anticipating the pleasures of the two of you "becoming one."

- Freely share all of yourself with one another.

Involving All Five Senses

Sexual closeness is often enhanced as more of the five senses are involved. Remembering that we see, touch, taste, hear and smell—get creative about involving more of your senses. To stimulate your creativity consider the following possibilities:

- Sight—soft lighting, intimate sleepwear, undressing one another

- Touch—body massage, bubble bath, different sleepwear fabrics, satin sheets

- Taste—soft kisses, fruit drinks, body lotions

- Hear—pleasant background music, sound tracks of surf or nature, soft whispers to one another

- Smell—scented candlelight, perfumed bath oils and powders, colognes and perfume

Take turns initiating and leading in your next two times of physical intimacy—each experimenting with involving all five senses. Use the Love Map exercise above to guide discussion.

CHAPTER THREE

Dimensions of Intimacy

Phil and Susy's Journey

When I arrived in Viet Nam I was assigned to a machine-gun team led by a battle-hardened soldier named Ralph. Ralph was the best machine-gunner in our outfit. We made an interesting team: one white, one black; one well-to-do, one middle class; one who had *inherited* social prestige, the other who *fought* for it. Staying alive required teamwork and unity despite our differences. Many times Ralph's keen knowledge of war led us out of a near fatal position. But there came a time for me to reciprocate.

During a mission on November 7, 1967, Ralph and I were manning a position at the forward perimeter. The enemy attacked and soon a third of our company lay dead or wounded. Before we knew it, Ralph and I were caught in a crossfire. Over the roar of the automatic weapon fire, Ralph screamed, "Downer, I'm hit!" Instinctively, in the midst of enemy fire, I jumped up to help him. Actually, the bullet had only pierced his uniform but for a moment he thought the bullet had gone through him. He was okay and we both survived that night. In the midst of the battle he learned about me what I already knew about him—that I was willing to risk my life to save his.

The warrior in every man would like to be courageous, loyal and steadfast in battle. I exuded that kind of loyalty to a man I had only known for four months. However, to my wife, the only woman I've ever loved, I had forsaken courage and become a coward. I was totally selfish. My selective memory only recorded my wants, needs, and point of view, constantly ignoring Susy's. I risked my life for a fellow Marine, but I would not lay down my rights for my lifetime partner, my wife. Even after becoming a Christian, I still often sought what was best for me and would plan and operate as though I were a Marine unit of one man. Quite often, men want to survive the war with valor and succeed in business with recognition, but too often we ignore the most important challenge—the spiritual war being waged against our family. We devote ourselves to everything other than God's priority for us—being faithful husbands and fathers.

Ralph and I were single-minded because we had a common goal of fighting well and surviving. The fear of death was our ever-present reminder that we had to work together. In a strange way, war can unite two vastly different people. Ralph and I also shared our hopes and dreams of what we wanted to do when we returned to the "real world." Emotional bonding occurred as Ralph comforted me when John, a fellow Marine, fell on top of me riddled with bullets. And I, in turn, comforted Ralph when a booby trap blew off Willie's legs. Although we came from backgrounds where the races didn't mix, Ralph and I transcended superficial differences as we shared each other's food, provisions, ammo, and foxholes without a second thought.

Living Vulnerably—A Prerequisite for Intimacy

Yes, I felt close to the men in my unit—a varied compilation of men who had agreed to a 13-month hitch with the fighting

Marines in Vietnam. And yet I found it difficult to share spiritual, emotional, and physical intimacy with this person with whom I had agreed to a "lifetime hitch." Emotional intimacy was difficult for me because in order to share my deep needs, passion, and vision, I'd also have to share my fears, weaknesses, and hurts. I had been taught to keep them to my self because "big boys don't cry." To me, physical intimacy just meant sex, which I pursued eagerly. But I ignored the caring touches, affectionate embraces, and tenderness associated with balanced physical intimacy. Men need to recognize that not only did some of God's greatest servants show tears and admit to weaknesses, but Jesus himself wept. He was truly acquainted with sorrow and grief, and when He hurt, He didn't just "stuff it." As followers of Christ, we too need to express our emotions and be vulnerable.

One of the greatest generals ever to walk the face of the earth, one who stood with great courage against impossible odds, was willing to admit weakness and failure. His name? Joshua.

> *"Then Joshua tore his clothes and fell facedown on the ground before the ark of the Lord, remaining there till evening. The elders of Israel did the same, and sprinkled dust on their heads. And Joshua said "Ah, sovereign Lord, why did you ever bring this people across the Jordan to deliver us into the hands of the Amorites to destroy us? O Lord, what can I say, now that Israel has been routed by its enemies"* (Joshua 7:6-8).

Joshua's honest prayer in which he confessed weakness, helplessness and humility, was heard by the Lord. God responded, "Rise up! The victory will be yours."

Following the example of Jesus and Joshua, we must be willing to share all of what's going on inside—our pain and our successes. In this chapter we'll explore these "dimensions" of intimacy and discuss practical "how-to's" of intimacy according to God's design.

The Priority of Marriage Intimacy

Marriage intimacy powerfully impacts the effectiveness of a man's witness for Christ. Each day brings new reminders that only as man's marriage and family are enjoying God's intended intimacy, is there the "platform" for broader ministry to other people.

My friend, Carl, had high hopes that his leadership team would become an effective combat unit in the battle for winning and discipling business men, their wives, and families in his large metropolitan area.

However, after getting the leadership team together, Carl recognized that these men were not ready, willing, or able to take on a vision of reaching their city for Jesus Christ, because, in different ways, the majority of the team had serious marital problems. Some were indifferent toward their wives, and others were too preoccupied with business and ministry to be the effective husband and father God called them to be. Before these men could reach their city for Christ, they needed to focus on their marriages. To ignore the problems in their marriages would undoubtedly lead to failure as they attempted to be salt and light in their city. After spending over a year in a marriage study, Carl now has a team of men who are willing and able to impact their world.

Intimacy Developed in Small Groups

Susy and I are involved in a regular marriage intimacy home group. Our small group has become much deeper and closer than a typical Bible study with friends. We have shared the deep issues of life with one another, and now feel that we have a community of believers to which we could bring any problem and find love, truth, empathy, wisdom, and godly support. These groups are also very effective tools for reaching unbelievers. In these groups you have the closeness everybody looked for (but didn't find) in the fraternity and sorority houses. These groups are based upon several premises:

- People must be honest, willing to share, and even willing to say when they're not willing to share.

- Everything shared must be held in confidence.

- The group should have a sustained membership, without a lot of change, and meet regularly (at least once a month and probably twice or more a month is ideal).

- The focus should be on Christ and His work in our lives and marriages.

- His work should not just be *studied* but also *applied*.

- The group should be fun.

After focusing on marriage and family, these groups are a perfect place to begin a lifestyle evangelism study course called "Living Proof I" which will equip the group to find common ground and build relationships with unbelieving friends, and through those relationships allow God to reach them for Christ.

David and Teresa's Reflections

What Phil has shared is absolutely true. If a man or woman wants to be effective in ministry, the first priority must be his or her marriage and family. Let's further explore the dimensions of marital intimacy.

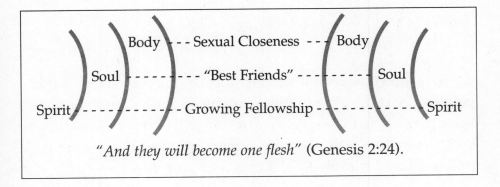

"And they will become one flesh" (Genesis 2:24).

Dimensions of Marital Intimacy

For relationships to be knit closely together in marriage or in families, sharing must be encouraged. "Closeness" doesn't just automatically happen because we have the same last name or live under the same roof! "Becoming one" in marriage involves the freedom to share *all* of oneself—spirit, soul, and body.

The chart on the previous page illustrates how a husband and wife can develop marital intimacy in three dimensions. Marriages need nourishment and attention in each of these three areas. Just as we need air, food, and water to be healthy physically, our marriages have essential nourishment needs. A growing, healthy, and balanced marital relationship is one where each partner is enjoying the abundance of intimacy—spirit, soul, and body.

Often, couples may enjoy a certain level of spiritual compatibility, have a tolerable friendship, but have a problematic sex life. Other couples might enjoy a growing friendship and a satisfying sex life, but have no real spiritual closeness. Marital happiness is achieved when all three dimensions are constantly being nourished and experienced.

Spiritual Oneness—Saints Enjoying Fellowship

To achieve spiritual oneness, each partner must have a personal, vital, and growing relationship with Christ, and then learn to relate to their spouse on a spiritual basis. A good place to begin is to pray together. If either partner is uncomfortable praying aloud, simply hold hands and pray silently.

Another way to develop spiritual oneness is to begin a joint prayer list and share together in the blessing of intercession and answered prayer. Other ways to develop spiritual intimacy may include discussing selected Scriptures together, ministering to others, and attending or teaching a Bible study together.

Soulish Oneness—Best Friends

The soul realm involves the mind, will, and emotions. Closeness is developed as thoughts are shared and time is given in the loving act of attentive listening; emotions are identified and openly shared in a receptive and understanding environment; and a closeness of will is realized as common interests are shared, mutual goals are identified and achieved, and oneness in decision-making is practiced.

Sexual Oneness—Lovers

Physical closeness requires open communication, a priority time commitment, and the freshness of creativity. Plan a weekend away without the children. Plan two sexual times together, just to focus on "giving" to your spouse, not taking.

Marital Intimacy Inventory

After you've taken a few minutes to reflect on your relationship with your spouse, indicate your perception of your degree of intimacy in the three areas of spirit, soul, and body.

Place an X on the scale below to signify your view of the relationship.

   1. The **spiritual** dimension of our relationship is:

Lacking in intimacy 1—————————5——————————10 *very intimate*

What aspect of your spiritual relationship would you most like to see changed or improved in your marriage?

_____

_____

   2. The **emotional** or friendship dimension of our relationship is:

Lacking in intimacy 1—————————5——————————10 *very intimate*

What aspect of your emotional relationship would you most like to see changed or improved in your marriage?

_____

_____

   3. The **physical** dimension of our relationship is:

Lacking in intimacy 1—————————5——————————10 *very intimate*

What aspect of your physical relationship would you most like to see changed or improved in your marriage?

_____

_____

Encouraging Vulnerable Communication

"...*perfect love casts out all fear*" (1 John 4:18-19). The "perfect" love of this passage is God's love—sacrificial, giving, and filled with initiative. As believers, we have received His divine love.

Much of what hinders vulnerability is rooted in FEAR—fear of being rejected or misunderstood, fear of inadequacy or retaliation. As we share His agape love with spouse, children, and others, it ministers freedom from fear. A very practical experience of this freedom comes as we engage in intimate communication.

Since God's perfect love is sacrificially given and takes initiative, one way to encourage deepened communication is by ministering reassurance such as the following:

- I want to reassure you of my commitment to listen to your heart, your feelings, and your needs in order to better know you and love you.

- I will make our sharing times a "safe place" for you to express your most intimate feelings. I commit not to withdrawal, reject, or criticize.

- I'm committed to keep our intimate sharing times confidential—just between you and me, and never to use what you share against you in any way.

- I see the importance of us sometimes needing to agree to disagree.

- I don't need you to "be me." I want you to have freedom to "be you" and all God desires for you to be.

- As I identify barriers within me during our sharing, I'm committed to address them, resolve them, and remove them so they'll no longer be a hindrance to our sharing.

- Realizing my need to be responsible for my emotions and behavior, I will not blame you or rationalize my behavior.

- When I let you down in some way and hurt you, I'm committed to bring healing and resolution as God sorrows my heart and I seek forgiveness.

- I want to reassure you of my commitment to better love you unconditionally. This is best demonstrated when, even though I may be disappointed or hurt in someway, I still lovingly give to you anyway.

- I'm committed to you and our relationship, and want to more consistently verbalize and demonstrate my care and love for you.

We will not sense the oneness in our marriage that God intends until we develop intimacy in all three dimensions: spirit, soul, and body. One out of three or even two out of three is insufficient. The following exercise will help us further explore what it means to become one as friends, lovers, and saints.

Take a minute to reflect back on these ten specific statements of "reassurance" and identify one or two you want to verbalize to your spouse this week.

Biblical Perspective

LOVE YOUR SPOUSE— SPIRIT, SOUL, AND BODY . . . BECOMING ONE AS SAINTS, FRIENDS, AND LOVERS

The three dimensions of intimacy relate to the three different "parts" of a human being: *"May God himself, the God of peace, sanctify you through and through. May your whole spirit, soul, and body be kept blameless at the coming of our Lord Jesus Christ"* (1 Thessalonians 5:23). It shouldn't surprise us that the Triune God who manifests Himself as Father, Son and Holy Spirit would likewise create us similarly "complex!" This complexity is compounded as two become one in the marriage relationship. Three uniquely different Greek words for love reinforce these dimensions of intimacy.

Saints Sharing Fellowship

> *"Agape" is shown through its action, initiative, commitment and giving.*

- **Agape** is used in the New Testament to describe the attitude of God toward His Son (John 17:26), toward humanity (John 3:16), and toward those who believe upon His Son (John 14:21). "Agape" is then used to convey God's desire that believers share this love with others—including spouses and children (John 13:34). "Agape" is shown through its action, initiative, commitment, and giving—not through its "feeling." "Agape" is an expression of God's Spirit and it is impossible to "produce" through self-will.

When two saints share fellowship, we see two recipients of transforming grace living in the awe and wonder of being loved by their Creator (John 1:16); two mere humans experiencing together the inexpressible joy of living today as children of God, partakers of the divine nature (2 Peter 1:4); two aliens and strangers walking in this world, but not of this world (1 Peter 2:11, John 7:16), laboring together as ambassadors for Christ; being transformed together into HIS image (2 Corinthians 3:18, 5:20); longing together for His soon return (1 John 3:2).

Study Questions

Pause and reflect about how God has abundantly expressed his agape love toward you. God has . . .

_____

_____

How could this type of love be better expressed in your marriage? I could . . .

_____

_____

Friends Sharing Friendship

- **Phileo** is distinguished from agape in that it speaks of tender affection and represents the emotional aspect of a relationship. Phileo speaks of two hearts knit together in the tenderness of mutual companionship. A descriptive characterization would be to affectionately CHERISH a special person.

Two hearts stirred with a cherishing of one another—this dimension provides the emotional content. Sometimes "up" and sometimes "down," these feelings remind us that this relationship is active! Alive! And changing! Common interests and goals are identified and deepened as mutual support is given; communication grows through open expression and vulnerability. Thoughts linger over the specialness of one another; two people have become "best friends."

> *Phileo speaks of two hearts knit together in the tenderness of mutual companionship.*

Study Questions

Recalling that Abraham was referred to as a "friend of God," write about how your friendship with the Lord might be deepened. (see John 15:13-15).

_____

_____

_____

What practical steps could you take toward becoming "best friends" with your spouse?

_____

_____

_____

Lovers Sharing Passion

- **Eros** is the word from which erotic comes; it speaks of sensual fulfillment and the physical pleasures of sexual expression. A God-given boundary to confine these pleasures to the marriage relationship is given often in the Scriptures.

> *"Eros" is the word from which EROTIC comes.*

Physical excitement, expectation, and arousal prompt a desire for marriage partners to "become one flesh" (Genesis 2:24). Physical attraction is involved and anticipation of physical togetherness grows into passion; thoughts of physical oneness stir a desire to touch and to verbalize; a mutuality of sensitive "giving" to the passionate needs of another unites two friends as lovers.

Reminded that it was God who created sexual intimacy for marriage, how might a couple's spiritual oneness and friendship be related to sexual satisfaction?

_____

_____

_____

What additional sensitivity, care, initiative, and giving might you express toward your spouse to deepen sexual intimacy?

_____

_____

_____

Experiencing Biblical Truth

MARRIAGE "STAFF MEETING"

"Do two walk together unless they have agreed to do so?" (Amos 3:3).

D eveloping and maintaining marriage and family intimacy requires that a husband and wife spend quality, consistent time together. The external stresses of work, carpools, child raising, and checkbooks need not take their toll on marital "oneness" if couples will take the time to "manage" family events before they "manage" you! Even Jesus, during His public ministry, found it necessary to consistently withdraw from the crowds and spend time with His disciples for special times of sharing and encouragement.

It's inconceivable that a successful business could operate without regular staff meetings. Why then do most families try to operate without a regular time of planned communication? If it works in business, it will work for the family.

Here are some *characteristics* of a successful Marriage Staff Meeting.

1. **Schedule the time**—don't leave it to chance! Preferably, the staff meeting will be a standing appointment, occurring at the same time and the same place each week. Perhaps a good time would be over lunch on Thursday, or Tuesday night after the children are asleep, or during Saturday morning breakfast. Some couples' schedules are

such that the time has to change each week. If so, prioritize scheduling the staff meeting for the coming week.

2. **Prioritize the time**—as much as possible, make it "inviolate." Once the time is scheduled—protect it! Treat the appointment like it's the most important item on your schedule—because it is. Prioritizing the Marriage Staff Meeting will produce a renewed sense of closeness (one wife cried with gratefulness when her husband remembered their staff meeting and turned down a golf date).

3. **Protect the time**—prevent interruptions and distractions. Find a quiet place at home, or if necessary, meet away from the home and office. Avoid phone calls or visitors if possible.

A fearful thought for many couples may be "What in the world will we talk about?" a productive staff meeting might have this agenda:

1. **Consider calendar coordination**—look ahead to the coming week. What's planned? What's the children's schedule for the week? Who's working late? What social activities are scheduled? Operate from a principle of agreeing on time commitments which affect the entire family before making these commitments. Plan your next couple date and your next family outing. You'll even find that there's often great value in calendaring some of your lovemaking times!

2. **Listening to one another**—one spouse or the other may just need to talk. When listening, establish eye contact and give undivided attention. Be quick to offer comfort,

encouragement, and support. Avoid giving advice, arguing, belittling, teaching, or lecturing. Be open to share hopes and dreams, feelings and insights about recent moodiness, and concerns and fears about the marriage, kids, money, and the future. The power of giving undivided attention allows you to enter into another person's "world" and really get to know them.

3. **Discuss family goals**—monitor their progress. As marriage communication deepens, written annual goals need to be developed for the family and broken down into quarterly/ monthly target dates. Goals and plans could be developed in these areas: marriage, social, financial, personal, family, educational, spiritual, and professional.

- Does the budget look tight this coming week or month? If so, how can we all help?

- What's our next planned major household expenditure and how could we all better contribute to bring it about?

- Have we scheduled our family vacation? Reservations made? Itinerary set?

- Have we decided on some new couple friends we want to get to know this year?

- How are our personal goals progressing—reading, diet, exercise, hobby—and how can we encourage and support one another?

- What aspects of church life do we want to be involved in this next quarter?

- What's the next fun marriage get-away we have planned?

- What projects can we plan which focus on sharing Christ with our neighbors?

4. **Discuss parenting plans**—if you don't become united on parenting issues, the kids will "divide and conquer!"

- Discuss significant disciplines issues; what seems to be working and what doesn't?

- Plan family times together plus quality time for each parent with each child.

- Discuss and agree upon parenting responsibilities and schedules for the next week. Who's needing help? Who's needing a break from the kids?

- What goals seem reasonable for our children this quarter in the areas of behavior, attitude, and responsibilities, and how can we work together to achieve them?

5. **Engage in productive "feedback"**—lovingly share areas of irritation, hurt, and disappointment. In an intimate relationship, there will be the freedom to, "*Speak the truth in love*" (Ephesians 4:15). A Marriage Staff Meeting provides a neutral setting in which touchy issues can be honestly shared in an atmosphere of acceptance and teachability. For instance, you might need to share:

- "I sure miss being alone with you, could we plan a date together?"

- "It would mean a lot to me if we could remain in agreement in front of the kids—and discuss any differences privately."

- "Sometimes it seems your initial response to situations is negative. Could we talk about why that is and discuss how I could be helpful in encouraging optimism?"

- "Last Tuesday I felt embarrassed when . . . . Could we talk about it?"

6. **Share words of appreciation**—for "who" your spouse is and "what" he or she has done. Use your weekly Staff

Meeting as a reminder that your spouse is a blessing to you! They do have good qualities! For instance, you might share:

- "Thanks for your help this week with the kids."
- "I was reminded this week of how much I appreciate your diligence is seeing that things get done around the house."
- "You are a very giving person, and it really showed this week when you . . . . "
- "I love you, just for who you are."

Establishing and maintaining a meaningful, weekly Marriage Staff Meeting will be one of the most important steps you take in pursuing wholesome and intimate marriage and family relationships. Conflicts, hurts, and misunderstandings will be resolved, and a oneness will develop, allowing you to experience the joy of "walking together" according to Amos 3:3.

Praxis

INTIMACY EXERCISES

Sharing Your Wishes

During your next Marriage Staff Meeting, try this exercise. It will help you identify and share areas in which you think the relationship could be improved through vulnerable sharing.

1. List up to six "wishes" relative to your relationship—be specific and positive. Examples: I'm hoping you can become more comfortable initiating affection with me. I would enjoy regularly scheduled "dates" together at least twice a month.

"Wish List"

_____

_____

_____

_____

2. Share your lists with your spouse. Sharing "wishes" helps avoid the destructive cycle of:

• Having expectations and anticipations (i.e., wishes) of another person.

• Not communicating these wishes.

- Becoming hurt or angry when these expectations aren't met! This isn't fair to either person.

3. Exchange lists. It will help you remember your partner's wishes. Begin working on areas that your spouse wants changed.

Learning to Identify People's Needs by Listening to What They Say

We all have important intimacy needs. These needs are built into the DNA of the human race, and they serve as catalysts for our motivation and they strongly affect our behavior. Many people are unaware of these needs in their lives and therefore don't know how to correctly express their needs when they are neglected. Even if we acknowledge our neediness, we often forget to properly express our needs to our loved ones.

Listed below are some phrases you might hear from your spouse, children, or friends. Beside each phrase, write down the need that's being expressed by each statement. Possible needs are: acceptance, affection, appreciation, approval, attention, comfort, encouragement, respect, security, and support.

- "You're too busy."
- "Look what I did."
- "Do you mind asking my opinion?"
- "Will you always love me?"
- "I just can't do this."
- "I feel out of place."
- "I've had a bad day."

- "I feel like a failure."
- "Could we spend more time together?"
- "I'm really upset!"
- "Hold me."
- "Would you help me?"
- "I have a big nose."
- "What do you think of what I've done?"
- "I can't do anything right!"
- "I've had it!"
- "You're always making all the decisions."
- "I just want a place we can call home."

Try using this exercise to prompt discussion of individual intimacy needs during a Marriage Staff Meeting or during a family night. This exercise is from the Intimate Life resource entitled, *Top Ten Intimacy Needs*. To order, see the information pages at the end of this book.

CHAPTER FOUR

High Performance, Damaged Emotions

Phil and Susy's Journey

I remember the day my father, Sam Downer, and I met Jim Ling, the "L" behind the giant LTV conglomerate, on an elevator. It happened to be the day that LTV filed for Chapter 11 bankruptcy protection. My father, a senior vice president with LTV Aerospace, said, "Good morning, Jim, how is it going?" With an air of confidence, control, and outward calm that defied the newspaper headlines I had read that morning, he said in a firm tone, "Fine, Sam, fine, all things considered." I thought to myself, "Wow, what a man, what a rock, what a tower of strength. That's the way I want to be." Here was the ideal man: perform but don't feel.

But my concept of the "ideal man" started developing many years before that elevator ride. While growing up, I remember an "Ozzie and Harriet" home by day, but fighting, crashing sounds, and angry voices at night. Our home was filled with strife and turmoil, but everyone pretended that everything was fine. I unknowingly embraced the misconception that pain and problems were to be stuffed. Again, the subtle but ever-present message was "perform but don't feel."

It wasn't until I buried my dad that I first learned that although he had been a very successful businessman, he had been fired from three different jobs during his career as he made his way to the top of the corporate ladder. I know Dad must have experienced much pain through those years, but he never told anyone. Words like *failure*, *can't*, *hurt*, and *need* were simply not a part of our family's vocabulary. The hallmarks of our house were pride, accomplishment, strength, coolness, and confronting the next challenge. Even while watching a touching scene on *Wagon Train*, *Gunsmoke*, or *Bonanza*, Dad and I would respond with humor or sarcasm, always hiding our emotions.

"Big boys don't cry" and "Marines don't retreat." That was my training, that was my conviction, and those were lies! After becoming a Christian many things changed, but the firewall around my emotions remained intact. Occasionally I would express emotion privately with God in prayer. But those times were few and far between.

My lack of emotion made me unable to relate to others on an emotional level. Several years after becoming a Christian I was the leader of a weekend retreat where several men were to share their life experiences. As one man was "rehearsing" the talk he was to make at the retreat, he shared how one of his four daughters had died from a dreaded disease. He very honestly described the heartbreak, the pain, and the helplessness he felt about the situation. When he finished, I was the first one to speak. Instead of sharing words of comfort, I piped up with my analytical mind, and said, "Well, Keith, that was good, but I really think you could sharpen your focus by using a few more verses, and there were a couple of other points that you left out of the suggested outline . . ." and I droned on with my heartless, emotionless analysis. I totally missed the message. I was so consumed with the details and mechanics of his speech, I completely missed hearing his hurting heart. My response only added to my friend's pain and sorrow.

On another occasion, one of my fellow attorneys came to me after being humiliated in the courtroom. He too was hurting but, true to form, I started to rattle through my analysis of what he had done wrong and how he could improve on his courtroom technique. My friend didn't hear a word I had said. I'm sure that he felt like I was only interested in his performance, not his pain. After that incident, he never confided in me again, except to share his victories, and only from a distance.

As Christians, we often act as though we are robots, incapable of feelings. Then we try to reach out to a broken-hearted generation and we wonder why we are so ineffective in our ministry. It's true that the gospel contains the facts about Christ's life, sacrificial death, and resurrection. But it's possible to keep that information in the mind and never have it take the 13-inch plunge to the heart. There must be an experiential and emotional aspect of relating to Christ as Lord and Savior. But sadly, we Christians often approach the lost world with a façade of perfection, an arrogance of presuming to have all the answers, and an unwillingness to get close, be vulnerable, and to hurt, bleed, and feel with men and women.

Another example of this is when my spiritual father, Jim, took me on a follow-up visit to see a man who had shown interest in the gospel after attending a CBMC meeting. Jim was thrilled as he watched me share my testimony and then take Aaron through the "Steps to Peace with God" booklet which explains the gospel. I then proceeded to ask Aaron if he would be willing to pray to receive Christ, and after we talked for a few more moments, I led him through the sinner's prayer and Aaron prayed to receive Christ! After the prayer, I glanced up and noticed Jim quietly wiping away a tear from the corner of each eye. As we walked back to my office, Jim was leaping for joy and praising the Lord but I analyzed the situation in a rather ho-hum attitude of, "Well, we did what we were supposed to do, and it worked."

As Jim and I continued to meet, the Lord began to show me that I was only focused on objectives, goals, truth, and methods for taking truth to people who needed it. But I really lacked compassion, empathy, and a gentle, listening spirit—essential qualities for impacting a hurting world. I realized that my emotions had been damaged, beaten down, and suppressed for most of my life. As we will explore in this chapter, my "emotional cup" was so full I found myself constantly escaping into performance and activity, seeking to control most everything and everyone around me. And when control was lost, anger came forth, wounding the ones I loved and was seeking to minister to.

> *My "emotional cup" was so full I found myself constantly escaping into performance and activity, seeking to control most everything and everyone around me.*

On the second night of our honeymoon I saw a side of Phil that I didn't know existed. He lashed out at me with uncontrollable anger. Frankly, neither one of us can remember what the issue was, but it was something insignificant over which I had no control. I cried myself to sleep that night for the first time in my life. Hurt, anger, and fear began to accumulate in my "emotional cup" and eventually my love for Phil began to grow cold.

From that point on, divorce was always in the back of my mind. However, I chose to stick it out for several reasons, none of which are very laudable. One reason we didn't divorce is that I hated to admit that I had made a mistake in marrying Phil. My self-centered pride in the fact that "no one in our family has ever been divorced" actually provided protection for us until Christ entered our lives and began to make some real changes. Also, I loved law school and law practice, and they provided a strong diversion from our marital strife. Thirdly, to Phil's credit, he was always sorry for the trouble he brought to our marriage and really tried to change, although without Christ that was impossible. His sincere apologies would endear him to me and I would think, "maybe this time he has really changed." I also didn't want to divorce Phil because deep inside I knew he loved me and my rejection of him would have been devastating.

There was one other reason—I would not have been welcomed home without Phil. Throughout my growing up years, my mother and father modeled commitment, even though they came to Christ about the same time Phil and I did. They were raised by godly parents whose principles and practices permeated their lives. Although I didn't know the Bible verse, I knew that I was supposed to leave them and become one with Phil. My pride prevented me from sharing with mom what I was going through and I was also reluctant because my parents had taught me that divorce was not an option.

David and Teresa's Reflections

Phil and Susy experienced a lot of hurt, Phil from his family of origin and both of them in their marriage. And hurt which is not properly dealt with accumulates! Let's explore how this happens, the symptoms we might exhibit when we get emotionally full, and the joy which comes from being healed.

Healing Emotional Pain

To hurt is to be human! No one likes to hurt, but the issue is not *if* we will be hurt, but *when, how much*, and *by whom?* Trying to eliminate or minimize our vulnerability to pain simply makes us impersonal and cold. The more invulnerable we become, the more impersonal and "machine-like" we become. Machines don't hurt, but people do. And God created us that way. God created us with emotional and relational needs and with them comes the inevitability of pain as they go unmet.

The issue then is what have I done with the pain? Have I resolved the pain? Or minimized and denied it? Healthy marriages heal and resolve inevitable pain rather than ignoring the pain or retaliating as a reaction to it. In the same way, the functional family heals inevitable hurt and provides an open/approachable environment in which this takes place. The dysfunctional family refuses to deal with family pain and instead of an open and approachable family environment, common family rules would be "don't feel," "don't trust," and "don't talk"—particularly about problems or pain.

Common Objections to Dealing with Pain

"It was so long ago."

"You can't undo the past."

"Time heals all . . . doesn't it?"

Many find themselves seemingly trapped between an unchangeable past and fear of change in the present. The issue is not how long ago the pain occurred but rather is the pain still alive within you? Time is a necessary ingredient for healing but not a sufficient one—more is needed! Has the sun gone down on your anger for years and years (Ephesians 4:26)? Has the fear which was not from God been removed? (2 Timothy 1:7; 1 John 4:18-19)? Have you found freedom from inner

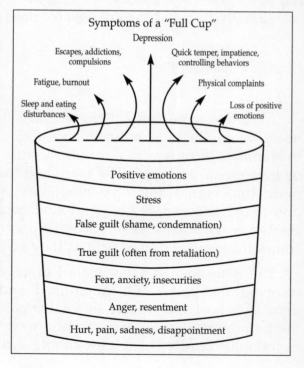

Symptoms of a "Full Cup"

Depression

Escapes, addictions, compulsions

Quick temper, impatience, controlling behaviors

Fatigue, burnout

Physical complaints

Sleep and eating disturbances

Loss of positive emotions

Positive emotions

Stress

False guilt (shame, condemnation)

True guilt (often from retaliation)

Fear, anxiety, insecurities

Anger, resentment

Hurt, pain, sadness, disappointment

shame (condemnation) and has the God of all comfort been allowed to comfort your hurt (Romans 8:1, 2 Corinthians 1:4)? Surely part of God's abundance for us is to remove the "sting" from the memories—the sting of anger, fear, shame, or hurt (John 10:10).

Before continuing, review the emotional cup chart and reflect on the following questions:

1. What overflow symptoms (temper, escaping, loss of positive emotions, etc.) do you exhibit? What symptoms does your spouse exhibit?

_____

_____

2. What unresolved hurts might be unresolved in you? In your spouse?

_____

_____

3. What anger might still be present in you? In your spouse?

_____

_____

4. What guilt do you sense over ways in which you've hurt your spouse?

_____

_____

Better Understanding Emotional Pain

Hurt or Anger—Two Sides of the Same Pain

Consider the pain which comes from rejection, ridicule, and marital infidelity. First there is a deep sense of hurt and loss (sadness, vulnerable feelings of a trust betrayed). Next we normally have feelings of anger, which often "cover" the feelings of hurt. The hurt feelings leave us violated and saddened and we suffer a diminished sense of "self" and are vulnerable to more pain. We feel so exposed that anger rises up to protect us. For many, the angry feelings are so automatic that there is no connection made between hurt and anger. Feelings of loss, and the vulnerability surrounding them, are tender feelings—but few can tolerate such vulnerable pain, so anger toward another rises up to distract and defend us. Thus, we hide our vulnerability and loss by being angry!

Hurt Involves a Loss to be Mourned

Human hurt is often defined as a violation of trust that results in a loss of something deeply personal. Related to human intimacy needs, hurt is associated with the loss of these needs being met—rejection rather than acceptance, neglect rather than attention, abuse rather than security. The pain of personal loss must be felt, shared, expressed, validated, and then comforted. Even unhealed hurts from the past must still be mourned.

Anger Wears Many Masks

The anger of unhealed hurts may be exhibited in a variety of ways. Among them are: impatience, quick-temper, depression, addictions, mistrust or suspicion, self-pity, and jealousy, plus certain passive-aggressive behaviors like procrastinating, avoiding, silence, and sarcasm. The process of healing must involve "working through" and releasing the anger.

Healing Marital Hurts Which Hinder Oneness

Hurts don't simply "go away." Time doesn't spontaneously heal resentment and trying harder doesn't erase guilt. The Bible, however, does not leave us without instruction on these struggles. Prayerfully consider the following admonitions as you prepare for follow up "homework" with your spouse: **Unresolved Anger**—Anger, bitterness and resentment require forgiveness. *"Let all bitterness and wrath and clamor and slander be put away from you . . . forgiving each other . . . ."* (Ephesians 4:31-32). **Unconfessed Guilt**—Unconfessed guilt from either active or passive retaliation requires confession. *"If we confess our sins, He is faithful and righteous to forgive us . . . ."* (1 John 1:9). *"Confess your faults to one another and pray for one another that you may be healed"* (James 5:16). The Experiencing Biblical Truth exercise included at the end of this chapter involves a marital project for healing unresolved hurts. The project places a high priority on the following principles:

Personal Responsibility

I must give an account of myself, not others—to God (Romans 14:12). Otherwise I live in a world of rationalizing, justifying, and blaming: "I wouldn't do that if you wouldn't . . . ."

Accountability to God

Hurting my spouse also "hurts" God and needs His forgiveness. It's sobering to realize that my selfishness, my unloving attitude, or my abusive and demeaning words were exactly why Christ had to die for me!

Confession of My Faults as Wrong

Quit confessing your spouse's faults and confess your own! "I was wrong" is much better than saying "I am sorry," since "wrong" tends to convey more responsibility, remorse, and repentance. The word "confess" means to "agree with," and God says these things are wrong.

Requesting Forgiveness—"Will You Forgive Me?"

The vulnerability of this confession conveys important humility and challenges a spouse with the responsibility to forgive.

"Forgiveness is a Choice—Not a Feeling!"

The Bible admonishes us to "put away" anger, wrath, and bitterness. Forgiving one another is a command to choose to forgive (release, turn loose of). Seal this choice by verbalizing your forgiveness: "I forgive you." Forgiveness is also an issue of stewardship: first we receive God's forgiveness and then we are challenged to share it with others.

Prayer Together Encourages Oneness

After confession and forgiveness, begin experiencing the intimacy of prayer together by holding hands and praying silently together.

New Memories Begin Replacing Old Ones

Old memories of hurt are now being "renewed" with new memories of your spouse confessing wrong and requesting forgiveness; new memories of you verbalizing "I forgive you"; new memories of sealing this healing time with prayer. *"Be transformed by the renewing of your mind"* (Romans 12:2).

Staff Meeting and Family Night Ideas

Schedule a time when you and your spouse can identify hurts and receive God's forgiveness. Refer to the "Healing Family Emotional Hurts" material (see the Experiencing Biblical Truth exercise at the end of this chapter) and then schedule a time to finish the exercise on confession and forgiveness.

Discuss the need for a family time of healing hurts (particularly with school age children and adolescents). If significant hurts exist between children and parents they don't simply go away! Schedule a family night to introduce the Healing Hurts exercise. Give each member a week to work through identifying hurts and gaining God's forgiveness, and then schedule confession and forgiveness for the next family night with parents making their apologies first (father leads).

Biblical Perspective

GODLY SORROW PRODUCES REPENTANCE

In a day when true life-change seems elusive, and any Christ-like distinction seems lost in secular culture, the fact that godly sorrow produces repentance is hopeful, good news. In the midst of continuing to *"do what I do not want to do"* (Romans 7:16), this promise regarding repentance is refreshing. The focus of Paul's burden for the Corinthians is not the outcome of repentance but rather the godly sorrow that actually produces (prompts, brings forth) genuine repentance. Before there's the external evidence of a changed life, there's the internal work of godly sorrow. A deep, emotional work of the heart must precede a change of behavior, attitude, and action. In his first letter, Paul challenged the Corinthians to a brokenness of heart, and in this second letter he rejoices with them in the blessed outcome. It's a surprising and emotional journey. It's also a very intimate journey as the Father reveals His pain to His children.

The Reality of Godly Sorrow

In contrast to the sorrow of this world, godly sorrow is timeless and eternal. In this world we experience tribulation and trials; struggles and losses take their toll. We constantly deal with the reality of rejection, regrets, disappointments, and pain, but we're not left alone in this journey because we have a Great High Priest who has gone before us (Hebrews 4:15) and who was acquainted with grief (Isaiah 53:3). Through the provision of divine comfort, we experience blessing in our mourning (Matthew 5:4) as it comes through Him and others (2 Corinthians 1:2-4). Still, this sorrow, as deep and penetrating as it is, remains common to this world and this life.

So what can we say about this godly sorrow that is not of this world? It is a response on our part to the knowledge that we have grieved God's heart. His sorrow can be revealed, shared, and imparted to the attentive hearts of His children.

> *It's a certain promise, a bold declaration— godly sorrow produces repentance!*

Study Question

Imagine that one of your dearest friends is about to share with you some of the things that have broken his heart, causing him deep sorrow. Encourage him to share with you his pain.

_____

_____

_____

The Reason for Godly Sorrow

Godly sorrow speaks of His pain—the pain of a Father rejected in eternity past by His created hosts (Isaiah 14:12-14), betrayed in the garden by the "very good" of His creation (Genesis 3), and repeatedly forsaken by His people (Exodus 32:7-10). Surely there is a sorrow-filled heart behind these words: *"Then the Lord saw that the wickedness of man was great on the earth and that every intent of the thoughts of his heart was only evil continually . . . and the Lord was sorry that He made man on the earth and He was grieved in His heart"* (Genesis 6:5-6).

To experience godly sorrow is to share in the Father's pain, the pain of a loving Father who for us would:

- Watch Him who knew no sin . . . become sin (2 Corinthians 5:21).

- Allow the perfect One . . . to be wounded, bruised and chastised (Isaiah 53:4-5).

- Hear His only begotten Son utter these words: *"My God, My God, why have You forsaken Me?"* (Matthew 27:46).

> *As we consider God's sorrow, our hearts should soften in sadness and grow quiet in brokenness as we consider our contribution to His pain.*

As we consider God's sorrow, our hearts should soften in genuine sadness and grow quiet in brokenness as we consider our contribution to His pain. Worldly sorrow focuses on our grief, what "we" did. Likewise, condemnation produces a type of sorrow, but it's a sorrow focused on "how terrible I am." But, godly sorrow shatters that self-focus as our heart ponders what we've done to the Father, His Son, and the Holy Spirit.

Study Question

Write about your heartfelt emotions concerning the Father's pain and rejection—particularly as you recall the Father hearing His only Son cry, *"My God, My God, why have You forsaken Me?"* What do you feel for the Father?

_____

_____

The Receiving of Godly Sorrow

The Father vulnerably reveals His heart, His pain—but not to the flippant or to those who are busy or preoccupied. He only trusts His sorrow-filled heart to those who can be still enough to know Him, patient enough to wait. "Sorrow" is not a "heady" thing to be dissected, discussed, and debated as doctrine. It's a personal thing between the Father and a loved one, a tender issue of the heart, an emotional issue of the soul.

> *It's a personal thing between a Father and a loved one, a tender issue of the heart, an emotional issue of the soul.*

It comes by way of the Spirit's conviction and my confession. Only the Spirit can convict (John 16:8), and only I can confess (1 John 1:9, James 5:16). The Holy Spirit will fulfill His role, convicting me of selfishness, a critical spirit, pride, and disrespect—specific offenses toward God and others. And then comes my part which is genuine confession. This means agreeing with God about my selfishness, criticism, pride, and disrespect as the Father says. More than mere intellectual agreement of wrong or a volitional voicing of regret, "to confess" is an emotional issue of godly sorrow. In the stillness of time and the quietness of things divine, my heart cries out in agreement with the Father's sorrow:

- Your Son was wounded for my transgressions . . . my selfishness and pride.

- Your Son was bruised for my iniquities . . . my critical spirit and disrespect. *"Against You and you only, have I sinned"* (Psalm 51:4).

- It was because of my sin that you had to hear those soul-piercing words, *"My God, My God, why have you forsaken Me?"*

Heartfelt confession will produce godly sorrow. No longer will there be self-defense, pretense, and posturing—only a broken and contrite heart. Entering into the intimacy of His suffering eliminates the "heady" pursuits to "understand" and to be "understood."

Study Question

Write from your heart concerning your response to the Father's pain:

_____

_____

> The "love of Christ that constrains us" (2 Corinthians 5:14) is the power that will change us.

The Results of Godly Sorrow

The results from such an encounter burst forth like fragrant blossoms on a well nurtured plant. The results, both internal and external, are not manufactured, forced, or produced by a "grit-your-teeth and bear it" type of obedience. They come humbly, gently, and supernaturally. The *"love of Christ that constrains us"* (2 Corinthians 5:14) is the power that changes us.

Because confession frees us of guilt, the first result is grateful rejoicing. Godly sorrow produces a joy in being forgiven and a grateful thanksgiving that ushers me into worship.

As to my guilt—*"The Lord was pleased to crush Him . . . He would render Him as a guilt offering"* (Isaiah 53:10).

As to my sorrow—*"Deliver me from guilt, O God . . . then my tongue will joyfully sing of Thy righteousness"* (Psalm 51:14).

As to my grateful thanksgiving—*"O Lord open my eyes that my mouth may declare Thy praise . . . for the sacrifices of God are a* *broken spirit, a broken and contrite heart"* (Psalm 51:15-17).

Godly sorrow also produces repentance, a genuine change of heart and direction that makes me more and more like Christ. It's a lasting impression on my life that I've been with Him; having entered into the fellowship of His sufferings, having shared intimately with Him in his sorrow, I can never be the same again.

> *"Deliver me from guilt, O God . . . then my tongue will joyfully sing of Thy righteousness"* (Psalm 51:14).

Study Questions

Write about your gratefulness:

_____

_____

_____

Write about your anticipated areas of repentance and change:

_____

_____

_____

Special Note: For some, this may be the first time you have personally associated your sin with Christ's death. By faith, if you will receive His forgiveness, He will cleanse you. Ask your spouse, pastor, group leader, or Christian friend to share with you how you can know Christ and the full pardon of sin. (You may also see Appendix A, *Steps To Peace With God.*)

Experiencing Biblical Truth

HEALING FAMILY
EMOTIONAL HURTS

*Here are six progressive steps which will lead
to emotional healing.*

1. Identify Hurt

Alone, list ways in which you have hurt your spouse and children. For instance, "I've been: selfish, critical, negative, insensitive, disrespectful, verbally abusive, unsupportive, ungrateful, unfaithful, rejecting, unforgiving." Specific hurtful events, fights, arguments or "scenes" may also need to be confessed.

_____

_____

_____

_____

*"Get rid of
all bitterness,
rage and anger . . . .
Be kind and
compassionate to
one another,
forgiving
each other . . . ."
(Ephesians 4:31,32).*

2. Gain God's Forgiveness

Confess to God and receive His forgiveness. 1 John 1:9 says, *"If we confess our sins, He [God] is faithful and just to forgive us and to cleanse us from all unright-*

eousness." Example: "God, I have deeply hurt You and my spouse (or child) by being selfish, critical, negative, insensitive, disrespectful, verbally abusive, unsupportive, ungrateful, unfaithful, rejecting, unforgiving. This is very wrong and I ask You to forgive me. Thank You for doing so and I ask You to change me into the kind of person you created me to be."

3. Confess Wrongs and Choose to Forgive

Together, share your lists and request forgiveness. James 5:16 says, *"Confess your faults to one another and pray for one another that you may be healed."* (We encourage husbands and fathers to confess first.) Example: "I've seen that I've hurt you deeply by being selfish, critical, negative, insensitive, disrespectful, verbally abusive, unsupportive, ungrateful, unfaithful, rejecting, unforgiving. I have been very wrong. Will you forgive me? ("Wrong" is better than "sorry" since confessing means "to agree with" God, and God has said these things are wrong.)

4. Respond: "I forgive you"

Remember: Forgiveness is a choice, not primarily a feeling! The question is not, "Do you feel like forgiving?" but rather, "Will you? Will you release (drop) the hurt?" Only then will anger dissipate and new feelings come! Also remember that you have first been forgiven by God—you now have the privilege of sharing some of His forgiveness with others.

Other areas to confess: It might be important to ask, "Are there other major hurts that I've not seen that need my apology? Please share them with me so I can confess them now and ask for your forgiveness."

Next: Wife shares her list (followed by children sharing theirs if this is a family session).

5. Embrace New Memories!

Exchange lists and tear them up! Philippians 3:13 says, " . . . *forgetting what lies behind and pressing forward to what lies ahead."*

Start the "forgetting" process with a focus on this new memory of forgiveness as lists are exchanged and destroyed. (Some people burn them!)

Additional suggestions: Hold hands and pray (even silently), thanking God for His forgiving you, changing you, and healing your marriage and family.

6. Establish A New Habit!

"Let not the sun go down on your anger" (Ephesians 4:26). Confession to God and others whom we have hurt along with forgiving others who have hurt us must become a daily habit if intimacy is to be maintained. Otherwise your emotional cup will again be filled with hurtful emotions.

Praxis

QUESTIONS FOR INTERACTION

Incorporate these questions in your upcoming Marriage Staff Meetings

- Where did you live between the ages six and twelve?
- What person or place was the center of emotional warmth or security for you in early life?
- When, if ever, did God become more than just a word to you?
- When did He become a living person to you?
- What is the most exciting thing going on in your life right now?
- If you could arrange things in your life in any way you wanted them, what would you change?
- Do inside or outside forces cause you the most trouble?
- What four words would you use to describe yourself? Which one is best?
- What word would you like others to use to describe you?
- What questions would you most like to ask God?
- Whose approval is most important to you?
- What age would you prefer to be and why?
- Are you more like your mother or father?
- Name two qualities you like best about yourself.

- Name two qualities you do not like about yourself.
- Jesus Christ thinks that I am _____.
- Write down a quality that you like about your spouse. Share.
- What is the best thing that has ever happened to you?
- What is the worst thing that has ever happened to you?
- Love means _____.
- What is, or was, your nickname and why?

CHAPTER FIVE

Affair-Proof Your Marriage

Phil and Susy's Journey

The man who discipled me was far from perfect, and yet he is one of the most godly men I've ever known. I could say the same about my spiritual grandfather, Dave, and my spiritual great-grandfather, Joe. A common characteristic each of these men share is a growing, honest, intimate relationship with their wives. It seems to be a common denominator among most men who are used greatly in God's kingdom. Obviously, none of these marriages is perfect, but each exhibited a firm foundation of security that served as a powerful example to Susy and me.

As young Christians, Susy and I were discipled by godly believers; me by a physician named Jim, and Susy by a woman named Liane. Jim and his wife, Mary Gail, were so close to one another that I felt totally comfortable calling Mary Gail and leaving her a detailed message about what was going on in my life. As Liane, Jim and Mary Gail parented us, they were transparent about their problems, pressures, and failures. They didn't simply teach us the Scripture, they also lived their lives honestly and openly before us. Through their examples, we learned many valuable lessons about to how to affair-proof our marriage.

Guard Your Marriage with Love

As I reflect back on the example of these godly marriages, I am drawn to a passage of Scripture that I have poured over many times through the years—1 Corinthians 13. Various times in my marriage, I've had to focus directly on the principles in this Scripture, and at times, I've even carried 3x5 cards with each of the characteristics of love written out with an empty box next to it. At the top of the card, I write two questions: "Does this quality characterize my relationship with my wife?" And, "Was this quality evident in my life today as I interacted with Susy?"

As Susy and I practice mutual giving— "*. . . honor one another above yourselves*" (Romans 12:10)—we find that our marriage is not only strengthened and enriched, but also guarded and protected.

In Paul's definition of love, he gives us seven things to do (commands of commission) and eight things to avoid (commands of omission).

Things To Do—Love Is . . .

• **Patient**. Have I been patient in my marriage today? Why am I in a hurry when the Lord has promised me sufficient time to accomplish all He wants me to do (without neglecting or mistreating my marriage)? Why do I sometimes show more patience to total strangers than I do my wife who has devoted her whole life to me?

- **Kind**. Have I been kind today? Susy doesn't care if I'm rich, famous, muscular, or perfect, but Susy has a right to expect me to be nice to her.

- **Rejoices at right**. Oh Lord, help me to focus on our blessings and not complain (Philippians 2:14).

- **Bears all things**. With Christ's help (Philippians 4:13), there is no challenge that comes my way that I cannot overcome.

- **Believes all things**. The Lord has given us confidence that He has a great plan for our lives and He will reveal it in Scripture. Also, do I believe in Susy's hopes and dreams? Am I supportive of her daily activities?

- **Hopes all things**. Through our suffering, he has given us endurance; through endurance He has given us character; through His character, He has given us His hope (Romans 5:1).

- **Endures all things**. When I think Susy has wronged me, I'm tempted to defend my "rights" but then I remember that I am to endure all things. With the Lord's grace, forgiveness, and help, we do have the ability to endure all things in our marriage.

Things To Avoid—Love Is . . .

- **Not jealous**. Why do I focus on others, instead of focusing on Him, and let that affect my relationship with my wife?

- **Not boastful**. Why am I so proud of myself when I'm really nobody without His loving grace in my life?

- **Not arrogant**. Why can't I learn from the humbling circumstances God has allowed in my life?

- **Not rude**. Lord, forgive me for not exercising control over my tongue.

- **Not insistent on its own way**. Jesus called me to serve, not to seek a position of authority. Am I willing to serve my wife and meet her needs?

- **Not irritable**. My irritability is usually caused by uncertainty and the loss of control, or to put it another way, fear. God has given me not the spirit of fear, but a spirit of power, love, and self control (2 Timothy 1:7).

- **Not resentful**. My resentment is, in reality, discomfort with and distrust of God's plan for me. Why should I question Almighty God's plan for me?

- **Does not rejoice at wrong**. Oh Lord, help me to be compassionate and not competitive, concerned for others and not eager to build myself up (Philippians 2:3).

Guard Your Marriage with Healing

When Susy and I have a disagreement, we try to quickly resolve the dispute with confession, repentance, and forgiveness. But years ago, I would use one of several "substitutes" for confession, which were not only ineffective, but caused further harm to our relationship.

- **Ignoring the problem**. This is where you "move on with a smile" as if there were no problem, leaving the issues undealt with and allowing the pain to fester and spread.

- **Giving an incomplete apology**. "Look, Susy, I'm sorry. Let's hug and move on."

- **Offering a "loaded confession."** "Honey, I'm sorry, but I would have been a lot more patient if you hadn't been late again."

- **Confessing the sin but ignoring the pain**. "Susy, I'm really sorry for my conduct. It was wrong of me to be rude to you; would you please forgive me?"

All along, Susy needed to hear a complete, appropriate apology.

"Susy, I'm very sorry I hurt you. What I did was wrong and I am really sorry for the pain caused by my rudeness with you. I need to work on trusting the Lord with my schedule and not take it out on you. Will you forgive me?"

In addition to our weekly dates, Susy and I have a real need to get off for longer periods of time for a one-on-one evaluation of where we are, where we've been, and where we're going in our marriage. It's during these meetings that God really works in our lives in a deep and decisive way. In your business, would you ever consider managing a department of salespeople without ever having sales meetings? Of course not. Then why would we not meet with the one who has invested more in us than anyone else on earth, outside of our Lord and perhaps our parents? This is why weekly Marriage Staff Meetings are so important, plus other times of "getting away."

Guard Your Marriage with Purity

Sexual sin is pervasive among men, largely because of how unguarded most of our hearts are. In working with men through the years, I have noticed that there are some common reasons why men fall into sexual immorality.

Secret Sins

Many men have developed secret habits that run deep and even continue after salvation and marriage. Although delivered from the power of sin, these men continue to indulge in pornography and other sins that lead them to greater moral failure. A surprising number of Christian men follow the pattern of Dan who, although he never technically broke his marriage vows through adultery, entertained a thought life that was shameful, destructive, and sinful. His thoughts went beyond momentary attractions or lustful thoughts to include fantasizing about women he met in business or saw in magazines. After years of harboring guilt and frustration, Dan came clean and confessed his destructive habit to his small accountability group. Dan was so disciplined in every other area of his Christian life that the men were shocked that he was so susceptible to immorality. They gathered around him, prayed for him, and kept him accountable to the Lord and his wife in thought, word, and deed. The great breakthrough for Dan was when his accountability group helped him make good on his promise to tell his wife about his problem. Sarah was first shocked, then relieved to understand why he was increasingly distant and finally she was able to forgive him, and appreciate his transparency and honest repentance. Through Dan's brokenness and resulting humility, Sarah found her husband to be more tender, open, and honest than ever before. Dan agreed with his wife and accountability group to make the same vow that Job made in Job 31:1.

No Fear of God

Carl was a mechanical engineer who testified as a forensic expert witness in construction cases. His life around the office was one of leadership, respect, and professionalism. He was also well respected in the community. His home life was relatively harmonious, except that he avoided one-on-one time with his wife and children. On the road, he lived a secret life after 8:00 p.m. After a tough day of work, he would go to his hotel and view various types of pornography. It was on Good Friday when the cross-examining defense counsel, seeking to impeach Carl's testimony in a case, showed all of Carl's hotel bills to the jury. The plaintiff's counsel objected to the introduction of inadmissible and irrelevant testimony, but the defense counsel persisted by pointing out that the hotel charges were included in the plaintiff's claim for damages. Furthermore, he wanted to show the jury that Carl, as an expert, was not credible or trustworthy. The judge bought the argument and ruled the evidence admissible, at which point the defense counsel paraded in front of the entire courtroom Carl's hotel bills which were riddled with area code 900 sex call charges and pay TV billings! The defense counsel was even prepared to prove, by hotel records, the titles and subject matter of the various movies charged to his account.

Christians are encouraged to get into small group Bible studies and accountability groups to face and analyze their weakness and failures from a biblical point of view.

Who do we think we're kidding when we think we can hide from God? He is omniscient and omnipresent, as well as perfectly just. God loves us and our purity a lot more than our reputation, so He will at times bring ruin to our reputation in order to expose our secret lives and call us back to Him. Carl's testimony was discredited, his reputation destroyed, and his marriage of ten years devastated.

One of the greatest values of the Lord's ministry through David and Teresa Ferguson and their marriage intimacy seminars is that Christians are encouraged to get into small group Bible studies and accountability groups to face and analyze their weaknesses and failures from a biblical point of view, and to knead into their lives godly solutions to the problems that create barriers and broken lives.

An Unbiblical View of Sin, or: "It Isn't So Bad Considering All The Things I Do Well."

Some men think that God grades on the curve. That is, if I'm not as bad as other people, I must be okay. This lie has kept many from salvation and prevented many Christians from experiencing the victorious life.

Jason was a senior vice president who managed the department of human resources for his manufacturing company in the Midwest. Jason was active in his church and community, and had a wonderful family. Jason enjoyed teaching large Sunday School classes and speaking to large groups of people; however, he avoided one-on-one discipleship like the plague.

True discipleship is analogous to parenting, as Paul indicated in 1 Thessalonians 2:7-8: *"We were gentle among you, like a mother caring for her little children. We loved you so much that we were delighted to share with you not only the gospel of God but our lives as well, because you had become so dear to us."*

One-on-one discipleship is not only the most effective tool to bring about change in individuals, but it is the method that God chose to bring about His kingdom (Matthew 28:19-20). Furthermore, discipleship is probably the best means of accountability a man can have. However, even in that setting, a man must be honest with the one he's meeting with. I have found that if men will lie to God and to themselves, they also will lie to other men.

This one-on-one discipleship was missing in Jason's life. He destroyed his marriage, not by having an affair, or engaging in pornography, but by giving away his affection and attention to those with whom he worked and counseled in his company. Jason was extremely effective in building teams. But in his textile manufacturing facility, they were primarily composed of women. He counseled his female co-workers about their marriages, children, social and love lives, and their workplace pressures. Jason swore he never touched another woman, but he periodically gave away his heart, affection, and interest to other women over the course of time. It wasn't until his wife confronted him with her great need for encouragement, attention, and affection that Jason realized the extent to which he had damaged their marriage. The situation was seemingly out of control. His wife, Jean, also worked for a large company, and in the sales department she was surrounded by men who were impressed with her business acumen, gentle spirit, and dogged determination. Jean got all the approval and attention she wanted—at work. She eventually had an affair with one of the men who reported to her. "The last thing I ever wanted was to be unfaithful to you!" were Jean's words, but she found her colleague's affection irresistible. Both Jason and Jean sinned against God and one another, Jason by being neglectful, Jean by being unfaithful.

Many of us grew up in an era where most moms stayed home and the dad worked. But that era ended with Norman Rockwell. We now live in a time when many women are in the workplace and they have to deal with all the same pressures and temptations that men do. Perhaps the greatest temptations come when their basic needs (such as attention, approval, acceptance, and affection) are met in the workplace when they should be met at home. Jason never went to bed with a woman other than his wife, but he sacrificed the sanctity of his marriage over a period of five years one conversation at a time.

Thou Shalt Not Steal

As I have worked with men around the country, I find a surprising number who must have watched too many reruns of the old TV show, *The Fugitive*. These men have a fascination with the daring, the offbeat, the high risk venture. Some of these men satisfy their desire for danger through risky business ventures or investments, but some men choose to fulfill this desire by flirting with "forbidden fruit"—they're fascinated with stealing someone else's wife.

Generally speaking, men don't read romance novels. But Trent did. He got into the habit of reading them on his daily train ride to work. Trent had grown up on the poor side of town and somewhere along the way, he believed the lie that it was okay to take from the "rich guys" as long as he didn't get caught. As a child, he got into the habit of stealing and as a teenager he was jailed for using drugs. When he came to Christ, he laid on the altar his lust for money, drugs, and power, and five years later was even active in ministry as a layman. He spoke to large groups and shared his testimony of how he was delivered from a life of crime and despair and delivered into God's kingdom through salvation by faith. But he never dealt with the root of evil in his life. Although he had a beautiful wife and three married daughters, he began a course of conduct in his office of subtle and then overt sexual harassment. As a career consultant in a Christian ministry, Trent had many closed-door, confidential meetings with his secretaries and staff. One by one, they would quit after only a few months of working with Trent. His wife noticed the revolving door in his office, with young females coming and going. Then one Saturday afternoon, Anthony, the husband of Trent's secretary, after almost breaking down Trent's door, accused him of assaulting his wife. It was only through the quick action of one of the neighbors that Anthony was kept from ripping Trent limb from limb. He was totally enraged after hearing his wife share the episodes of sexual harassment and physical assault she had endured working for Trent. One accuser's testimony might have been discredited, but seven other employees came forward with similar stories. It wasn't until halfway through the court case, brought by the women suing for damages, that Trent finally confessed to his sinful and unlawful conduct. Trent never overcame his temptation to steal that which was not his, and it virtually destroyed his life.

Greed

Solomon had a thousand wives and concubines. Obviously, he didn't need that many wives; he just wanted more. He seemed to have a problem with wanting to have "the most." He had the most wisdom, the most money, and the most horses, so maybe he couldn't stand the idea of not having the most women as well.

Tim was just such a man. He always wanted to have just a little bit more than everybody else. He didn't set his salary goals based on what he was worth, he just wanted to make more than the guy next door. He didn't care about close relationships with his children, he just wanted them to be the most involved and recognized kids in school. He didn't care about having deeply committed and godly friends, he just wanted to impress everyone in town. His desire for "just a little more" led him to a pattern of unfaithfulness in his marriage, and it was only after he lost his wife that he realized he had destroyed the one person who loved him for who he was as opposed to whom he knew and what he had. Greed is a great killer of the Christian life. And it can lead to another great killer—sexual immorality.

Escape

Some men are unhappy with their circumstances and attempt to escape in various ways. In Judges 4 there is an account of a man named Sisera who was fleeing the Lord's army. Seeking escape, he mistakenly went to the tent of Jael, a Kenite woman whom he did not realize was loyal to Israel. Feeling secure in his escape, he was even able to sleep in the comfort and security of her tent. But while he was asleep, Jael *"drove the peg through his temple into the ground, and he died"* (Judge 4:21)!

Men often try to escape the discipline of the Lord, and when they do, they experience tremendous pain and loss. Patterns of anxiety and fear in our lives can drive us to do the unimaginable. One of my prayers for purity in my own life is that if I ever dishonor the Lord, my wife, and family by sinning with another woman, that three things would happen to me: (1) everyone in the world I know would find out about it the next day, (2) I would contract every known disease possible from such a moral failure, and (3) I would wake up afterwards with a tent peg through my temple. The Lord has said our hearts are wicked and deceitful, and our desire to walk in purity must be accomplished by a reminder of the fact that God hates sin, there is no "safe tent." The eternal impact of a life well-lived is never worth sacrificing for a moment of pleasure. We must guard against and never give into the "just this once" lie of Satan.

David and Teresa's Reflections

Guard Your Marriage By Meeting Needs

Surveys consistently indicate that marital affairs are not primarily sexually motivated. The pain and guilt of sexual infidelity usually come as an acquaintance develops into a "friendship," emotional bonding is added, and flirtation and temptation follow The typical "attraction" is built not so much around the physical but the emotional. Significant emotional needs in the marriage are perceived as "unmet" and thus a vulnerability develops and looks for solutions.

Recall our previous marital truth: Basic Needs Unmet = Frustration. Frustration leads to vulnerability, and vulnerability can develop into an affair. Therefore it's important to understand your spouse's emotional-relational needs. With these needs "abundantly" met, your marriage is much more "affair-proofed."

Perhaps the most common justification for extra marital affairs is: "My wife (husband) and I don't ever talk anymore. I was just looking for some companionship."

This comment indicates that there are significant unmet needs in the relationship. For example, "We don't talk anymore" might really mean "I'm needing attention, understanding, or empathy." "Looking for companionship" might reveal unmet needs for support, appreciation, acceptance, or affection. It's our premise that when these significant emotional-relational needs are met, a spouse is much less vulnerable to other companionship.

As a role model of the relationship between Christ and the church, marriage is to portray a relationship built on giving to meet needs. Ephesians 5 speaks of Christ loving the church as He "gave Himself." There's great fulfillment in giving oneself and in sharing the comfort, love, and acceptance God has first given. As valid needs are met in the life of your spouse, marital intimacy and satisfaction are deepened.

Intimate Encounters—Key to Marital Closeness

Intimacy is developed and deepened as couples share experiences which draw them together. Intimacy doesn't just happen without effort, but neither can it be programmed to happen. Couples seem to grow in closeness, for example, as they encounter one another spiritually, emotionally, and physically. Such an encounter might be an ecstatic moment of common joy, a tearful sharing of genuine apology, an unhurried conversation, or an affectionate embrace. These intimate encounters help deepen marital closeness.

Intimate Encounters Include Three Dimensions—Spirit, Soul and Body

Spiritual encounters might include quiet prayer together or working together on a mission project—two developing genuine fellowship. A "soulish" or "friendship" encounter involves the mind, emotions, and will as thoughts and dreams are shared, feelings are mutually expressed, and common interests developed—two becoming best friends. Physical encounters involve caring touch, affectionate embrace, and passionate union—two becoming affectionate lovers.

Intimate Encounters Involve Four Ingredients

These four ingredients present a sound "strategy" for developing intimacy.

- **Affectionate Caring**—"I care for you." I want to know you; I'll be there when you need me—because I care for you.

- **Vulnerable Communication**—"I trust you." I am willing to vulnerably share with you my pain, fears, weaknesses, thoughts, dreams, and aspirations—because I trust you.

- **Joint Accomplishment**—"I need you." I can't do it without you, I love it when we do things together—because I need you.

- **Mutual Giving**—"I love you." I think more highly of you than I do myself; I want to meet your needs—because I love you.

A committed and sensitive partner will seek to abundantly give to his or her spouse's needs—not out of fear but out of the abundance of God's gracious provision. Happy need-meeting!

Biblical Perspective

TAKEN CAPTIVE BY HIS LOVE
2 CORINTHIANS 5:14

Everywhere we go, we cannot help but hear the human cry for liberty. However, we also find contradictions in this cry. Each day brings more controversy over rights and freedoms: parental rights versus children's rights, states' rights versus national priorities, abortion versus pro-life, discrimination versus reverse discrimination, freedom from moral decay versus freedom of expression, right to die versus personal responsibility. Our fast paced and media driven culture has seemingly brainwashed us into demanding our freedom at any cost.

> *"So if the Son sets you free, you will be free indeed"* (John 8:36).

The Paradox of Freedom

In our modern context, we can easily miss the biblical paradox of freedom. Christ often spoke of the paradoxical nature of His kingdom—lose your life and find it (Matthew 16:25), love those who despise you (Matthew 5:44), and die in order to bear fruit (John 12:24). But perhaps the greatest biblical paradox concerns "freedom." The paradoxical message is presented in various settings and uses a variety of analogies, but the message is clear: surrender to God's Spirit, God's Son, and God's love, and you'll experience true freedom: *"Where the Spirit of the Lord is, there is liberty"* (2 Corinthians 3:17), *"So if the Son sets you free, you will be free indeed"* (John 8:36).

In one of the most insightful passages on this paradox, we find Christ sharing the truth of finding true rest, saying, *"Take my yoke upon you and learn from Me"* (Matthew 11:29-30). Submitting to His yoke brings blessing. Somehow our yielding brings liberty as His yoke is easy and light. Only captivity to Christ brings true freedom.

Held Captive By Something

Scripture is filled with references to the pervasiveness of our captivity. As non-believers we once *"Followed the ways of this world and . . . the ruler of the kingdom of the air . . . ."* (Ephesians 2:2). The Greek word "sunecho" used in 2 Corinthians 5:14 to describe the "captivating," constraining love of Christ, is also used to describe being held captive by fear (Luke 8:37), by the crowd (Luke 8:45), and by enemies (Luke 19:43). Paul uses the same word to describe being *"torn between the two"* as he shares the dilemma of wanting to be with Christ yet remaining with the Philippians (Philippians 1:23). It seems that captivity is inevitable! But by God's grace we can choose our master. Will it be fear, the crowd, enemies, the course of this world? Or will it be the constraining love of Christ?

> *We can choose our master. Will it be fear, the crowd, enemies, the course of this world? Or will it be the constraining love of Christ?*

Study Questions

Pause and reflect on some areas of past captivity in which you now experience freedom.

_____

_____

What heart-felt emotions do you have on these areas of liberation?

_____

_____

Captivating Love is to be Experienced

Captivity is not an intellectual exercise or mental process. It is first and foremost experiential truth, an experienced reality that impacts one's total being. It's more than seeking to mentally comprehend the vastness of God's love only to be frustrated by our finiteness. So it is with the constraining love of Christ. It's more than choosing to tell others about this great love, as significant as this is. So what does it mean to be constrained by His love? To better understand and experience such constraint is to better comprehend true love as an issue of God's heart and nature rather than only an issue of rational truth. The declaration that *"love is from God"* (1 John 4:7) is a certain and secure rational truth. But to personally experience that this love was *"manifest in us . . . that God sent His Son to be the propitiation for our sins"* (1 John 4:9-10) makes it an issue of relationship, an emotional issue of the heart. I am, have been, and always will be loved by my Creator. How will my heart respond? To explore this issue is to explore experiencing His constraining love.

"Sunecho" also gives insight into the fullness of this constraint. The word seems to describe the believer's heart response to the Father's boundless love. The word is often translated "to hold," "to secure," "to control or empower." Could it be that:

- Thanksgiving for His unmerited love **holds** me in grateful obedience, freeing me from the pull of my sinful nature;

- Praise for His loving character **reminds** me of my secure future, freeing me from the fear of losing His love;

- Worship of the God "who is love," **empowers** my grateful stewardship of His love, freeing me from selfish preoccupation.

Notice that thanksgiving, praise, and worship are not merely passive intellectual musings, but experiences of the heart and spirit! Write words of:

Thanksgiving

_____

_____

Praise

_____

_____

Worship

_____

_____

Experiences of Captivating Love

It's His love that is constraining, motivating, and empowering. Therefore, we should find evidences of this divine love lived out in our lives.

- His love **initiates**—it moves first, never waiting around to be asked or invited. *"There is no one who seeks for God!"* (Romans 3:11), but rather, *"He came to seek and to save"* (Luke 19:10). Initiate, initiate, initiate toward those whom God has called you to love!

- His love **sacrifices**—it's free, but it's not cheap; it cost God dearly. *"God so loved the world that He gave"* (John 3:16). *"As Christ loved the church and gave Himself up for her"* (Ephesians

5:25). Sacrifice a little of your time, convenience, and self-interest in communicating His love toward others.

- His love **rejoices**—it gives with gladness, thrilled at the opportunity to care for others. *"And when he finds it (a lost sheep), he joyfully puts it on his shoulders . . . ."* (Luke 15:5). *"Selling their possessions and goods, they gave to anyone as he had need . . . with glad and sincere hearts"* (Acts 2:45-46). Rejoice often over the privilege of giving. Reflect often on the wonder of having something of eternal significance to share.

In an age filled with knowing about truth, rather than experiencing it, take particular note of the relational and experiential nature of His constraining love which initiates, sacrifices, and rejoices!

Study Questions

> *Rejoice often over the privilege of giving.*

What *initiative* could I lovingly demonstrate toward my spouse?

_____

_____

What love *sacrifice* could I make to bless my spouse?

_____

_____

What are a few ways my spouse brings *rejoicing* to my heart?

_____

_____

Experiencing Biblical Truth

MEETING YOUR SPOUSE'S NEEDS

Husbands, Minister to Your Wife's Need for Security

Security can be defined as "freedom from threats of danger or pain; to be safe and certain and sure of one's safety." The key issue in meeting a wife's need for security is to do what you can to remove her fears. For instance, a wife who fears that her husband's work is more important than she is, might feel insecure. A wife who fears that her husband is not totally committed to marital fidelity or permanence will naturally feel threatened. Countless fears will inevitably arise over the course of a marriage relationship and a loving husband can be actively involved in helping remove them, thus building a more secure relationship.

Husbands, complete the following exercise with your wife. As she shares, listen attentively and reassure her that you care.

Biblical Reflections

"*For God did not give us a spirit of timidity*" (2 Timothy 1:7).

"*But perfect love drives out fear*" (1 John 4:19).

"*Husbands, love your wives, just as Christ loved the church*" (Ephesians 5:25).

Better Understanding Her Need for Security

Noted below are several ideas to help deepen the sense of security in a marriage. Ask your wife to make two lists for you:

I'd love for your top 5 priorities to be:

1.

2.

3.

4.

5.

I often feel your top 5 priorities are:

1.

2.

3.

4.

5.

- **When you sense your wife's fears or insecurities, say—** "I can sense you're feeling fearful and I want you to know I'm committed to reassure you . . . I want to help drive out your fears."

- **Ask about her fears—**"Honey, could you share with me some of the things that you've recently been worrying about or fearing? I'd like to work on helping you with them."

- **Ask your wife how you can increase her sense of security—**"What could I do to help you feel more secure in our relationship? I really want to help."

- **Have weekly Marriage Staff Meetings—**Make it a priority to schedule a "talk" time with your wife each week (1 to 1-1/2 hours) to discuss plans, schedules, children, family needs, and anything else your wife would like to discuss. This time helps a wife feel more secure that she and the family are indeed very important to you.

- **Schedule dates regularly—**Schedule times when you and your spouse are doing something alone, just for fun, without children (that's family time), and without friends (that's social time). Give your wife something to look forward to; your initiating the plans helps her feel secure in your leadership.

- **Make 30 second phone calls—**"Hi, Sweetheart. I was just thinking about you and wanted to call to check on you. I love you and look forward to seeing you tonight." This communicates an important emotional message that says,

"Even though I'm working a lot and very busy . . . I'm thinking of you!"

- **Engage in vulnerable accountability**—Ask your wife: "What are some things I've been doing recently that irritate you? I want to work on changing some of them." Listen attentively without being defensive; pray about what is shared and then implement needed changes. A willingness to consider your wife's wishes for change helps communicate that she is a high priority to you.

Wives, Minister to Your Husband's Need to be Honored

Honoring your husband means to value him as an especially meaningful person in your life—your personal hero. It also includes honoring his wishes as you are sensitive in desiring to please him and honoring his decisions as you free him to lovingly lead you. Honoring your husband is a special ministry of love that requires a deepened work of faith.

Wives, complete the following exercise *with your husband*. As he shares, listen attentively and reassure him that you care.

Biblical Reflections

- " *. . . like Sarah, who obeyed Abraham and called him her master. You are her daughters*" (1 Peter 3:6).

- *"Be devoted to one another . . . give preference to one another in honor"* (Romans 12:10).

Better Understand His Need To Be Honored

Listed below are several ideas to help deepen your husband's sense of being honored.

- List below six areas of strength or positive character qualities you see in your husband

1.

2.

3.

4.

5.

6.

Now practice communicating your appreciation for these six items: (1) verbally when you're alone, (2) publicly when you're with others or, (3) in writing by a special love note.

- **Ask about wishes**—Honey, I want to better honor you as my husband—particularly in seeking to meet more of your special wishes. Would you share with me some wishes that I could help fulfill?

- **Talk about decisions**—"As I come to realize how much I need and value your leadership, I want to become more sensitive not to criticize or resist your decisions. Can you share with me decisions in which you'd appreciate more support?"

• **Make him "King For A Day"**—Schedule a surprise day focused on giving just to him; maybe breakfast in bed; a special card, favorite outing, favorite friends over, or just quiet "togetherness"—be creative and even romantic!

• **Brag and don't compare**—Emphasize his strengths and communicate appreciation. Don't tease him or attack him through comparisons with other men—co-workers, fathers, brothers, pastors, etc.

• **Don't sweat the small stuff**—Back off and let him make decisions and even mistakes. Let him miss an exit off the expressway or pick a restaurant with a long waiting line. Let him verbalize wild ideas without shooting them down!

• **"Date" him again**—Return to some of the little things he enjoyed while dating: sit by him, hold his hand, use his favorite perfume or special sleepwear, play "our song," etc. (Most men haven't grown out of these wishes!)

• **Be honest about your passive-aggressiveness**—What are some things you know he enjoys but that you withhold from him when you're angry? This inventory usually reminds you that you already know many of his wishes—the issue then becomes putting away anger (Ephesians 4:31-32) so you can be free to unconditionally love him.

Praxis

THREE PRACTICAL WAYS TO HELP "AFFAIR-PROOF" YOUR MARRIAGE

Couple Prayer Times

One recent survey indicated fewer than 15% of church-going couples pray together. Most of the reasons are obvious:

- I'm not exactly sure what to say.
- I would not pray as well as the Preacher.
- I might get corrected by my spouse!
- . . . and the list of excuses goes on . . .

One simple recommendation is this:

Spend a few minutes talking about things that matter:
- . . . concerns, hopes, dreams or fears
- . . . kids, work, money, feelings, or future events. (This might come at the close of a Marriage Staff Meeting or during the last minutes before sleep.)

Reach over and take one another by the hand (a husband's initiative here as leader seems appropriate). Pray together silently for two or three minutes (if you become comfortable praying out loud, fine and if not, fine). You'll sense an important spiritual closeness to one another and you may also find that emotional and physical closeness will follow.

Sharing Emotions

Each of us experience emotions. Some share their feelings openly while others hide them. Some seem overly sensitive to emotion, while others are unsure of what they feel. The same emotion can be expressed in greatly differing ways. For instance, loneliness for some might be expressed with sad withdrawal, while for others it might be expressed through endless conversation. A major ingredient in relational closeness is the open and constructive expression of emotion. The first step is to develop an emotional vocabulary. To encourage emotional sharing in your marriage, take turns naming as many emotions as you can.

Why is it important to identify emotions? One reason is that many times, emotions define for us major emotional needs: feeling unappreciated means we need appreciation; feeling rejected implies needing acceptance and feeling misunderstood implies the need for understanding.

Together, list at least ten positive emotions (excited, hopeful, etc.) and ten painful emotions (lonely, rejected). Then take turns sharing recent events in your lives and the emotions they evoked. For instance, a person might identify anger as a felt emotion, but in reality this anger might be the "sum" of feeling unappreciated, rejected, and misunderstood.

Marriage and Family Goal Setting

Without a Vision, People Perish—Proverbs 29:18

Every marriage needs a vision—a sense of direction and destiny; a guiding framework around which we can make decisions and distinct objectives toward which we can stretch.

Using the exploratory questions below, discuss each item and begin to identify specific goals you'd like to see accomplished:

- In what two key ways would you like to see me grow personally in the next year?

- How would you most like me to pray for you in the next few months?

- What is a reoccurring concern you may have about each of our children?

- What is an important item you'd like to see emphasized in our romance?

- What do you see as two of the most important challenges we may face this year?

- What improvements or changes would you most like to see around our home?

CHAPTER SIX

Blessed are Those Who Mourn

Phil and Susy's Journey

Because of the childhood pain I experienced, I developed a deep sense of loneliness and insecurity. On two occasions, Mom spent several months in a mental institution which left my older sister and me to fend for ourselves—alone. My sister tried to take care of me the best she could, but she was also dealing with her own feelings of rejection and hurt. She was in a more difficult position than I was because she was in high school and her friends were more generally aware of our family's problems. My three best friends, Steve, Ted, and Jimmy, nicknamed me "Pruner" which made me want to vomit every time I heard it.

By and large, I had to deal with my pain alone. As my trauma at home increased, my friends were embarrassed, our neighbors were shocked, my dad got even more busy at work, and no one from our church ever reached out to us. But there was one person who I knew cared about me, understood my pain, and accepted me for who I was—Mrs. McKay, my next door neighbor. She had even caught me doing a lot of bad stuff but genuinely forgave me. I never knew if she figured out that I was the one who cremated a dead cat in her incinerator, egged her house on Halloween, and raided her garage for pine boards for boats. But regardless, she always seemed to care. I always sensed her love and concern, often while I devoured another piece of her fabulous homemade pie.

I don't remember if she went to church or not and we never discussed religion, but as an accomplished opera singer, she had gotten her start singing hymns in the church. Mrs. McKay loved and cared for me during the most difficult time of my life.

Several years ago I talked with Mrs. McKay and shared with her how much she had meant to me and how I had found the ultimate cure for the pain, insecurity, anger, and bitterness that I had developed as a boy. As I sat in her home, I shared how I had come to Christ and then asked her if she would like to go through the gospel tract called, "Steps to Peace with God." (see Appendix A). She said she would. As we went through the Scripture, she would finish verses I had started to quote. When I looked surprised she said, "Well, I played piano in church when I was a child." She was then well into her 80's. When we got to the end of the presentation of the gospel, she said she wanted to pray to receive Jesus Christ as her Lord and Savior, and to my absolute delight, I had the incredible privilege of leading Mrs. McKay to Christ.

I'll always have a special place in my heart for Mrs. McKay because she was the only one who mourned with me as a child when I was hurting. Of course, as a young boy, I didn't know that what she was doing was technically called "mourning." All I knew was that it sure felt good. She allowed me to verbalize my hurt, frustration, and anxiety and then she responded with kind, gentle words. She didn't try to lecture me, and thank goodness, she never said, "Phil, big boys don't cry." Whenever I left her house, I felt comforted, blessed, and always full of pie!

Years later, I discovered what was going on in those meetings between a kind lady and the neighborhood brat—Matthew 5:4, *"Blessed are those who mourn, for they shall be comforted."* I mourned, Mrs. McKay comforted me, and I left feeling blessed!

David and Teresa's Reflection

Mrs. McKay met a very significant need in Phil's life—the need for comfort. In this life, hurt and pain are inevitable and comfort is the solution.

Before we discuss in detail, the biblical principle of mourning and comforting, we need to discuss the principle of emotional responding—responding to emotion with emotions.

Emotional Closeness—A Lost Ingredient

Our world emphasizes achievement and performance to the exclusion of emotional development. Young children do well enough learning to tie their shoes and count to ten, but who helps them identify and deal with their feelings? School age children usually begin a treadmill of endless activities—scouts, dance, sports, piano—but how do they learn to handle the normal rejections, fears, and disappointments of life? Adolescents often focus on athletics, academics, popularity or "crowd pleasing," but how are they healing their inevitable hurts?

Without developing an adequate feeling vocabulary or much emphasis on emotional sharing, adults often enter marriage hopeful of deep emotional closeness but are ill-prepared to engage in it. The friendship dimension of intimacy begins to suffer as feelings of love, romance, and affection diminish. Without adequate emotional skills, a couple copes the best they can, often content with just staying together. There's often a drifting apart into separate worlds—a husband absorbed in his business or hobbies and a wife escaping into the world of professions, being "super mom," or the endless activities of modern life. This drifting apart can bring further complications of increasing resentment, self-sufficiency, and heightened fear of rejection or abandonment.

Spiritual Complications

For many couples, this "coping" existence is made even more tragic by its contrast with their religious expectations and hopes. Much pretending often takes place because what is observed at home is so different from the Scriptural ideal proclaimed at church. Can I honestly be living a life which is *"thinking more highly of others"* (Philippians 3:2) and have it make such a small impact at home with my marriage and family? Can I genuinely be living in a way that is consistent with the grace of having been forgiven while at the same time harboring anger and bitterness toward a spouse or other family member (see Ephesians 4:31-32)? When a person's home is dramatically different from their spiritual values and teachings, feelings of inadequacy, guilt, and condemnation are usually added to the previous pain of loneliness, rejection, fear, anger, and bitterness.

Developing the Skill of Emotional Responding

At Intimate Life Ministries, we're often asked, particularly by men, "How can I get in touch with my emotions? Sometimes I feel emotionally numb and I know that this is hindering my ability to relate to other people, particularly my wife." Our answer to that question is to explain what we call "emotional responding." Simply put, emotional responding means that when emotions are shared, an emotional response is required. When the response to emotion is one of logic or facts, criticism or complaint, intimacy is hindered and couples and families begin concluding "we just can't communicate!" An emotional need must be meet with an emotional response. Learning this seemingly simple but profound principle can greatly enhance our relationships. Emotional closeness is a major part of being "best friends" with a spouse and is obviously a significant ingredient in sexual intimacy as well. Emotional responding is learning to respond to another person's emotions. If your spouse, child, or friend expresses an emotion, you need to answer him or her with an emotional response. It would sound something like: "I am so sorry you are going through that; that sounds so tough; I care about you a lot."

This is often very difficult for us to do because:

• We may never have developed a feeling vocabulary.

• We won't let our hearts feel what our heads know.

• It is easier to answer emotions with fact-based responses.

• We have no idea what emotional responding looks or sounds like.

In order to enhance your marital relationship, let's take a look at these four hindrances and learn how to correct them.

First, develop a feeling vocabulary. (You started a list of emotions in Chapter 5. Try to expand this list.) You might then spend time sharing as a couple or as a family. Here is an example of what emotional sharing may sound like, "Today, I found myself feeling _____ when _____ happened." This will help you develop a feeling vocabulary.

Study Questions

Recently I found myself feeling (some positive emotion) when . . .

_____

_____

Recently I found myself feeling (some painful emotion)
when . . .

_____

_____

In one sense, emotional responding is simply the
experiencing of Romans 12:15: *"Rejoice with those who rejoice;
mourn with those who mourn."* When you experienced the positive
emotion noted on the previous page, did you share it with your
spouse? Did he or she rejoice with you? When you experienced
the painful emotion noted above, did you share it with your
spouse? Did he or she mourn with you?

Second, learn to let your heart feel what your head knows. In
order to experience abundance and intimacy, we have to open up
to feelings. As individuals, we are wired to think, feel, and do.
Many of us don't handle the feeling part well.

Remember that Jesus experienced emotion. In the Upper
Room He wanted His joy to remain full in the disciples (John
15:11). He wept with Mary at Lazarus' death (John 11:35). In the
garden He said, *"My soul is overwhelmed with sorrow . . . ."*
(Matthew 26:38). Jesus experienced emotions, but did not let
them control Him. It is okay to experience emotions. It does not
make you weak. Spend time meditating on the sufferings of
Jesus (John 13:21, John 14:7-9, Matthew 26:38-39). Ask the Father
to open your emotions as you enter into the *"fellowship of Christ's
sufferings"* (Philippians 3:10). Coming to feel emotionally for
your Savior will prepare you to feel for those whom you love.

Third, emotion should always be answered with emotion.
Many times we answer with substitutes and they never work.
Some of those unproductive responses include:

- **Facts, logic, and reasons**—Someone has just said some hurtful things to you. As you tell your husband about it, he responds, "Don't let what she says bother you. You know it's not true."

- **Criticism**—Or he responds, "You sure are sensitive. Why do you let her get to you so easily? You really need to toughen up."

- **Complaints**—"It sure was stupid to let all those people know how easily she gets to you. I found the whole thing embarrassing. If you keep this up we won't have any friends."

- **Neglect**—"Well, I sure hope you can work it out. It's not my problem."

Fourth, what does emotional responding look and sound like? It always includes understanding, empathy, gentleness, reassurance, and confession if necessary. For instance, if your spouse is hurting, how does that make you feel? (Sad, compassionate, etc.) Use those feeling words to communicate to him or her how it makes you feel to see your spouse hurting: "It saddens me to see you hurt because I care about you; I have compassion toward you when you hurt because I love you."

The chart on the following page further explains the concept of emotional responding, illustrating some classic unproductive responses to emotional need or hurt. Such unproductive responses tend to be associated with unfulfilled or unhealthy relationships.

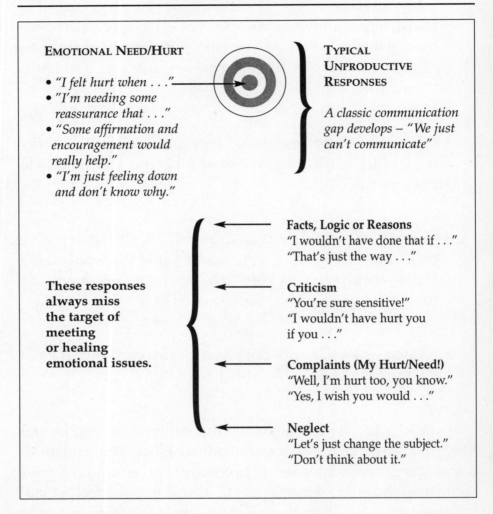

When we put emotional responding into practice, we experience Matthew 5:4.

- A person is hurting—mourning.

- Someone comforts them—comfort.

- The hurting person receives blessings, even when nothing external has changed. The thing that hurt may still be in place—but I'm blessed that you care! I'm not alone in my hurt!

This chart illustrates productive responses to emotional need or hurt.

EMOTIONAL NEED/HURT

- *"I felt hurt when . . ."*
- *"I'm needing some reassurance that . . ."*
- *"Some affirmation and encouragement would really help."*
- *"I'm just feeling down and don't know why."*

BRINGING:
- healing
- understanding
- fulfillment
- closeness

EMOTIONAL RESPONDING

Includes:
- understanding
- empathy
- gentleness
- reassurance

. . . and often times must include confession!

EXAMPLE PRODUCTIVE EMOTIONAL RESPONSES

- "I can really see that you're hurting."
- "I don't like to see you hurting."
- "It saddens me to see you so fearful."
- "I care about you and love you so much."
- "I'm committed to go through this with you."
- "I genuinely regret my part in hurting you."
- "Can you share with me how I've hurt you? . . . and how it made you feel? I want to understand and make it right."
- "I now see that I hurt you by my _____ and that was wrong of me . . . . Will you forgive me?"

Comfort is powerful. God tells us to *"mourn with those who mourn"* (Romans 12:15), *" . . . so that we can comfort those in any trouble with the comfort we ourselves have received from God"* (2 Corinthians 1:2-4), and that it is *"not good for man to be alone"* (Genesis 2:18). As we apply these scriptural principles to our lives, we will indeed experience the blessing of intimacy as our aloneness is removed through the caring involvement of others.

Biblical Perspective

TAKEN CAPTIVE BY HIS LOVE
2 CORINTHIANS 5:14

The Occasion of His Weeping—"When Jesus saw her weeping."

In a day when men's love has grown cold (Matthew 24:12), it's significant that we see Jesus as a caring, concerned friend.

Jesus was with those He loved. *"Jesus loved Martha and her sister (Mary) and Lazarus"* (John 11:5). Weeping is an appropriate response to a loved one who is in pain. When we rejoice with those who rejoice and weep with those who weep, love takes on an emotional dimension. More than simply "knowing" that we're loved, the emotional element allows us to experience "felt" love. For instance, a child may intellectually "know" that he is loved by his parents because they provide for him and protect him. But it's also important for the child to "feel" loved. Likewise, we know God loves us because He abundantly provides for us; but we more fully experience His felt love through His willingness to shed tears.

> *"When Jesus therefore saw her weeping and the Jews who came with her, also weeping, He was deeply moved in spirit and was troubled . . . . Jesus wept"* (John 11:33, 35).

This story also demonstrates Jesus' selfless caring. It was an occasion of sadness, loss, and grief that brought Christ's tears. But it was not primarily His loss, but that of another; not His grief, but Mary's. Shedding tears for another may be one of our most selfless acts of love—hurting that another is hurting; weeping that another weeps.

Study Questions

List other examples from the gospels when Jesus expressed comfort and compassion:

_____

_____

What does His example say about your need for comfort and compassion?

_____

_____

What does His example say about your need to express comfort and compassion?

_____

_____

The Example of Weeping

> **"He was deeply moved in spirit and troubled" (John 11:33).**

The gospels often speak of Christ being *"moved with compassion"* (Matthew 9:36, 15:32, Luke 15:20)—not just ready to give advice. A compassionate heart first communicates true care and concern. Then, from the security of a care-filled relationship, advice, instruction, and exhortation can be offered. The old cliché is true that says, "people don't care how much you know until they know how much you care." As Jesus weeps, we see an example of deep inward expression. Jesus' tears are an issue of the inner spirit, an expression of a troubled heart. Tears do not flow merely from man's intellect, right doctrine, or from a disciplined life of right living. Right "believing" and right "behaving," as critical and necessary as they are, will never be sufficient in expressing Christ-like gentleness, compassion, and tender care. Tears are an issue of the heart.

Jesus also demonstrates vulnerable self-disclosure. *"Jesus wept."* The caring, troubled heart of the Savior is disclosed. There's no self-protection or hesitancy from fearing others' disapproval. Not only has He come to know Mary's pain (and ours), but He also reveals His own. Since man's fall in the Garden, he has hidden, worn the mask, and played the games. But the last Adam, Jesus, forsakes all games and masks—He reveals Himself as all man and all God.

Study Questions

Discuss the significance of the following statement: "Right belief and right behavior are essential to Christ-like living, but they are not sufficient to fully express Great Commandment love."

_____

_____

Discuss what factors (childhood issues, cultural messages, examples) might hinder you from the vulnerable, self-disclosure of comfort.

_____

_____

Consider 2 Corinthians 1:2-4 and realize how God, as the God of all comfort, has comforted you. How is your sharing comfort with others being a good steward of what you have received?

The Miracle of His Weeping

The crowd was amazed when the carpenter from Nazareth shouted with a loud voice, "Lazarus, come forth." And they were no doubt shocked when he did! What an astonishing miracle—the rejected One from Nazareth raised the dead! But there were other miracles that day, perhaps less obvious but equally amazing.

Consider the miracle of God crying! Just as miraculous as a man raising the dead is a God who would cry. The Creator of the universe, the true God-man entered into the pain of an obscure family from Bethany—and cried. For every believer, there's the miracle of the empty tomb, but there's also the miracle of our great High Priest who can sympathize with us and enter into our sorrow. For every child of God, there's the sure promise of heaven but there's also the miracle of His daily attentive care, concern, and compassion.

The Miracle of Removing our Aloneness

Mary is no longer alone in her grief—the Savior has entered her world. Mary mourns the tragic loss of her brother, but the Savior's tears bring comfort and blessing to her heart. Even in her grief. *"Blessed are those who mourn for they shall be comforted"* (Matthew 5:4). But how can one feel blessed in the midst of grief, pain, loss, and mourning? As Christ's empathetic tears drive away Mary's aloneness, her pain subsides and her fear diminishes because of His love and concern. *"Perfect love drives out fear,"* (1 John 4:18) and there is no more perfect love than a God who cries for me and allows me to shed His tears for others. It is the wonder and beauty of "weeping with those who weep."

Study Questions

What impact do you experience emotionally as you meditate on the fact that Jesus is your Great High Priest, and that He hurts when you hurt and rejoices when you rejoice? How does that impact you emotionally?

_____

_____

Reflect on a time in your past when you received true comfort from spouse, friend, or family members and write about how your pain was turned into a blessing (Matthew 5:4).

_____

_____

_____

_____

Experiencing Biblical Truth

MEETING YOUR SPOUSE'S NEEDS

Spiritual Intimacy—Where to Start?

For most couples, physical oneness (sex) is relatively easy to assess or count, emotional oneness is somewhat difficult to grasp, and spiritual oneness is almost too vague of an idea to even discuss. Is spiritual closeness simply attending the same church or sitting together in worship services? Is it having identical beliefs or using the same Bible?

Tragically, for many Christian couples, their individual spiritual life may be maturing, but their spiritual closeness as a couple is more myth then reality. Here are some recommendations for improving spiritual closeness:

Where to Start Personally

Commit to one new spiritual goal

Couple closeness is founded upon two individuals each getting closer to God only to find that they feel closer to one another. Sample goals:

• Read through the entire New Testament this year (one chapter a day will more than do it).

- Memorize ten Scripture passages on communication (Ephesians 4:29, Proverbs 10:19, 12:18, 12:25, 15:1, 15:28, 16:23, 17:27, 19:13, 25:24).

- Establish a daily devotional time.

- Apply yourself to consistent Bible study. (See suggested resources at the end of this book.)

Where to Start as a Couple

There are two simple but effective ways to develop spiritual oneness:

- Pray together (see Praxis, Chapter 5).

- Read selected Bible verses and share insights. Choose a verse (for example Matthew 6:33: *"But seek first his kingdom and his righteousness, and all these things shall be given to you as well"*) and share what the verse means to you. Avoid criticism, arguments, or giving "my answer is more spiritual than yours" responses.

Emotional Intimacy—Where to Start!

Through Communication

Counselors often list as the top marital issues: communication, money, sex, and kids! Although therapy may be needed to deal with deeper underlying issues such as insecurity, fear of rejection, resentment, and childhood hurts—these top four issues are common "presenting" or surface problems. The couple may see one or more of these issues as a major stress in the relationship.

Fundamental among these four is the issue of communication since it obviously greatly affects a couple's ability to feel with the other three (money, sex, and kids). Each of us communicates not only through words, but also through actions, behavior, attitudes, and body language. Communication skills must be learned, improved and practiced.

There are several different types of communication:

- **Chit-chat**—"Hi, how are you?" "How was your day?" "When's dinner?"

- **Factual**—"Evan hit Liz today." "Your car's out of gas." "Do I have money in my account?" "I'm too tired tonight!"

- **Intimate**—Freedom to share dreams, hopes, fears, feelings and concern in an atmosphere of loving acceptance.

If the pulse of your marital communication is not as intimate as you would like, it is likely suffering from one of the following common hindrances to intimate communication.

- **Unavailable Spouse**—It takes quality time together to move past chit-chat. (Thus the importance of Marriage Staff Meetings, Chapter 3.)

- **Unhealed Hurts**—Why talk intimately with someone I'm still mad at! (Thus the importance of Healing Marital Hurts and forgiveness, Chapter 4.)

- **Unbridled Tongue**—Speaking before you think often wounds other people.

- **Unproductive Criticism**—Being criticized quenches intimate talk.

Communication doesn't just happen! The most common divorce pleading is "incompatibility," even for couples married twenty years or longer. Tragically it's possible to live in the same house, eat at the same table, and sleep in the same bed, but not really know one another. As a beginning point, you need a weekly Marriage Staff Meeting if you haven't already started this habit.

Physical Intimacy—Where to Start!

Improving the Quality!

Sex is often among the top four problems couples have and it's the quantity of sexual encounters that is the most frequent complaint. Tragically, couples have often come to define their sexual relationship in terms of numbers. How often do we have sex? How many times did one or the other reach orgasm? How much foreplay? How long did it last?

It's tragic to take God's beautiful and mysterious design for "two becoming one flesh" and reduce it to numbers. A fundamental error in marriage enrichment is to attempt to negotiate these numbers—comparing your sexual frequency with the "average" couple (whatever that is), or agreeing to trade two more sexual encounters per week for twenty more minutes of foreplay. (Or for one dinner date and cleaning out the garage!) The following is a much better approach.

Focus on Quality and Quantity Resolves Itself!

Here are some suggestions for improving the quality:

1. **Plan times together**—great stress and much anger comes from dashed expectations at the end of a long day when there's no mutual desire. (All of your sexual encounters should not be planned, but some should.)

- Calendar together some times during Marriage Staff Meetings.

- Part in the morning with tenderness, touch, and one of you expressing, "I'd sure like to be together with you tonight—let's plan on it!" (A big plus to arousal is anticipation—allowing yourself, through the day, to think of pleasant sexual times with your spouse.)

- Maybe it's time for: a night alone without kids, friends or other distractions; some unhurried lovemaking; a coupon special at a local hotel or trading out with a friend for overnight child care so you can be alone in your own house. A good recommendation would be to work toward one night alone for sexual rekindling every six months.

2. **Add variety to your lovemaking**—Sexual routine often produces boredom and disinterest. Consider the following:

- Vary the atmosphere through changing locations or times of the day; change the lighting or use candles; change lingerie or use sexy nightwear; change powders, perfumes, or aftershaves; add music.

- Vary the routine through changing sexual positions; change who initiates (trade off pleasuring one another); add a full body massage with baby oil or lotion; creatively be together other than in the bed!

3. **Communicate more openly**

- Sexual intimacy can't be a guessing game; two physically different people with differing personalities, backgrounds, preferences, and hang-ups must gradually learn to talk more openly about sexual oneness.

- During a relaxing massage of one another; give feedback as to good and great feelings.

- Read to one another portions of *The Song of Solomon*.

Praxis

EMOTIONAL RESPONDING

When someone is hurting, the only proper response is comfort. However, we are often tempted instead to offer unproductive substitutes such as: logic/reasoning, pep-talk, advice/instruction, minimizing, personal fear/anxiety, or a martyr's response. Review the following scenario below and discuss the six "unproductive responses" and the one "productive response." With each unproductive response, pause and reflect on how you might find yourself responding in this manner.

Setting

John and Suzanne have been married for ten years. Suzanne has just had an upsetting encounter with her aged mom who is in a nursing home. Upon arriving home, she shares with John the incident with her mom. The proper response to her disclosure about the hurtful and upsetting encounter is for John to comfort her. But instead, John gives various unproductive responses. Finally, he speaks words of genuine comfort.

Scene

(Suzanne and her mom are at the nursing home.)

Suzanne: Mom, you've got to eat! You can't go on like this. You're going to starve yourself to death.

Mom: I'm not hungry

Suzanne: Mom, don't be difficult. On top of not eating, the nursing staff says you've been staying in your room all day by yourself. You need to get out and make some friends. It would be good for you.

Mom: That nursing staff has been watching me like a hawk. They need to mind their own business.

Suzanne: They're just trying to help. They want you to get better.

Mom: They don't care about me—and neither do you!

Suzanne: Mom! How can you say that?

Mom: It's true.

Suzanne: It is not! I come to see you at least every other day.

Mom: Why not every day?

Suzanne: Mom, I've got three small children at home to take care of; sometimes I just can't get away.

Mom: Like I said, you just don't care.

Suzanne: Mom . . .

Mom: You go on now . . . come back when you can.

(Later in the day, Suzanne is at home, sharing with her husband.)

Suzanne: John, I'm so upset. I went by to see Mom today, and she refuses to eat her meals, she's driving the nursing staff crazy, and when I was about to leave, she said I don't care about her.

John: Sweetheart, I've told you before, old people just act like that. I'm sure if you were to take a poll of everyone who has a parent in that nursing home, they have the same problem. You need to face the facts, honey. It's just a part of the cycle of life; parents get old and they need to be taken care of.

Which unproductive response is this?

John: Sweetheart, remember we went through the same ordeal with my parents. I can remember getting so frustrated with my dad that I thought I was going to have to hire a fulltime nurse. And my dad wouldn't even go to a nursing home. He insisted on staying in his house. At least at the nursing home they fix meals for your mom, and they're available in case of an emergency. All in all, this is coming at a bad time for me; I'm really busy at the office, and I don't need the extra burden of having to deal with your mom.

Which unproductive response is this?

John: Wow, that's a pretty tough situation. But the whole world doesn't revolve around your mom. Let's not make a big deal about this; it's not the only thing going on in our lives. There are plenty of good things to concentrate on— Jimmy's t-ball game is this afternoon, and we're going off together next weekend. Don't let this one event get you down. What did you say was for dinner?

Which unproductive response is this?

John: Suzanne, that's ridiculous. You've been a wonderful daughter to your mom. No one would ever accuse you of being unloving or uncaring. You're one of the most caring people I know. Don't let it get you down! We've been through tough times before, and you handled them like a champ! I've no doubt that you'll do it again!

Which unproductive response is this?

John: Well, it's time we do something about it. Let's call the nursing home administrator and get her input. I'm sure this is not the first time something like this has happened. We might need to raise a little cain; remember the squeaky wheel gets the oil, and if you want them taking care of her, you're going to have to make some noise. Relative to the meals, believe me, your mom will eat if she gets hungry enough. Perhaps a change in diet would be good.

Which unproductive response is this?

John: That's bad news. We're already paying out the nose for nursing home care. If your mom gets to where she needs a personal nurse, the cost will sky-rocket. How in the world can we do that with all the kids' college? And with all the pressure I'm under at work, I really don't need another problem right now.

Which unproductive response is this?

John: That makes me so mad! She's just doing that to get attention. Why would she treat you like that? I feel like calling her out . . . .

The productive response:

John: Suzanne, I'm really sorry that you had a hurtful encounter with your mom. (John reaches over and holds Suzanne's hand.) It hurts me to see you hurt. I know you love your mom, and it's hard to hear her say things like that. Next time you go to the nursing home, let me go with you, just to give you support.

What makes this response so effective?

_____

_____

Study Question

After completing this exercise, discuss with your spouse which unproductive response you are most likely to slip into. Then pray together and ask the God of all comfort to use you on a more consistent basis to comfort others (2 Corinthians 1:2-4).

_____

_____

CHAPTER SEVEN

Leave Father and Mother

Phil and Susy's Journey

An explosion took place one morning in the Morris household when Pete told Jackie that he had been having an affair. In the midst of the argument, Pete even blamed his infidelity on Jackie's uncontrollable temper, and further accused her of being insensitive to his needs for attention and physical affection.

Soon after Pete confessed his infidelity, he flew to another city and tried a court case (and did a fairly good job of it). His callousness and lack of concern were evident signs of his hardened heart.

When Jackie first related this experience to me, she asked me not to tell Phil, being afraid it would ruin Pete's Christian witness. But later, with Jackie's permission, I shared it with Phil, and the two of us vowed to do our best to reclaim the Morris marriage. As Phil and I analyzed and prayed over their situation, we realized that they both shared the same problem. Their hearts were hardened to their sin. The primary question they faced was this: were they going to be willing to repent so that healing could begin?

Although Jackie had come to Christ at an early age, she grew up with deep insecurities and carried a lot of false guilt. As a result, the normal stresses and anxieties of each day quickly filled her emotional cup, at which point her anger would erupt. These outbursts of anger would occur even though she spent time in the Bible every day and faithfully attended Bible studies. Although she was a Christian, the hurt she sustained in childhood was slowly destroying her marriage. She had never completely left the pain of her past, so she was not capable of "cleaving" to her husband and becoming one with him.

When we first met with Pete, his main problem was an unwillingness to accept responsibility for his sin. He kept blaming Jackie. He not only resented her temper, but in one of our sessions, he confessed his anger with Jackie because she, like her mother, was not able to have children (Jackie had been adopted).

A breakthrough came for Pete when we shared with him Romans 14:12, *"Each of us will give an account of himself to God."* He realized that he alone was responsible for his infidelity and that it was sin Pete needed to confess. When he brought up Jackie's temper problem, 1 Peter 2:20 was our response: *"But how is it to your credit if you receive a beating for doing wrong and endure it? But if you suffer for doing good and you endure it, this is commendable before God."* Finally, they both took responsibility for their own sins and properly confessed.

If we had stopped at this point, their marriage would not have been completely healed. It was obvious that Jackie was really controlled by her past. Previously, Pete's anger and resentment toward Jackie had prevented him from having any empathy for what she had been through—he didn't even want to know. But after the time of confession and forgiveness, Jackie felt that she had a safe place in which to share her pain. For the first time in their married life, she sensed that her husband truly cared about her past hurts.

One by one, Jackie began to share the hurtful experiences of her past. It was not a pretty picture. She felt rejected by her father, inadequate with her mother, hurt by her parents' divorce (for which she blamed herself), and envious of other children who were not adopted. All of these issues contributed to Jackie's distorted view of God and herself. Her "full cup" produced many symptoms: at a young age, she learned to use her anger to manipulate people, and her anxiety produced a fear of failure which led to obsessive tendencies for perfection. She was always trying to change Pete in the same way her mother had tried to change her father, and she feared that Pete would reject her because she was childless.

What Jackie shared broke our hearts. As we imagined her as a small child, experiencing such pain and hurt, our hearts were filled with sorrow.

Amazingly, when Jackie shared these things with us, it wasn't in anger. She truly grieved her pain and loss. She mourned.

Our response? We comforted her. We didn't try to cheer her up, or explain away why these things happened to her. We didn't minimize her pain or spiritualize her loss, (*"And we know that in all things God works for the good of those who love Him . . . ."* Romans 8:28). We simply comforted her. We *"mourn(ed) with those who mourn"* (Romans 12:15). She was particularly blessed watching Pete, perhaps for the first time, understand her past and empathize with her.

Pete's sense of brokenness and repentance was further deepened as he came to better understand his wife. He realized how his infidelity had not only caused present pain, but had served to revisit unhealed pain. Jackie's vulnerability and willingness to expose her deepest needs, in turn, prompted Pete to be more open about his moral failures.

It took several sessions to deal with their most critical issues and, in a matter of months, their marriage had experienced a deep level of healing.

In retrospect, we had simply helped Jackie "leave" the pain of her past, so she could "cleave" to her husband. And just as Scripture promises, they were then able to "become one." *"For this reason a man will leave his father and mother and be united to his wife, and they will become one flesh"* (Genesis 2:24).

David and Teresa's Reflections

Yes, marital intimacy will always be elusive if we don't leave our family of origin. And this leaving involves several different areas. To illustrate, let's consider a hypothetical couple named Dave and Laurie and analyze their situation.

Dave and Laurie are having marriage problems. On the surface it appears that their problems are somewhat normal and predictable; their symptoms seem to be common problems that plague many couples. Laurie has occasional outbursts of jealousy and Dave responds by defending himself. Dave gets impatient with his wife's less than immaculate housekeeping, and Laurie feels frustrated, used, and unappreciated. Rather than facing these issues head-on, both Dave and Laurie tend to avoid them by escaping into their own activities. When Dave works too many hours at the job, Laurie just goes over to her mom's house and spends the evening talking to her mom and step-dad.

For years they've been refereeing their symptoms, but the problems just won't go away. A root issue is feeding the symptoms, and until it is properly dealt with, the surface problems may change slightly, but they won't go away.

There are three commands in Genesis 2:24, and their order is important. A husband and wife can't "become one" until they "cleave" to one another, and they can't cleave until they've "left" mother and father. Laurie and Dave's problems are rooted in the fact that they've not yet left their family of origin.

Leaving and cleaving involves at least four areas.

1. We must leave behind certain opinions and expectations about behaviors that we observed in our parents. This is the basis for Dave's misunderstanding regarding Laurie's housecleaning. Dave grew up in a home where "cleanliness was next to godliness." His mom was obsessive about house cleaning. When vacuuming the floor, she wasn't satisfied unless the vacuum cleaner's wheel marks were all parallel. She spent the better part of two days each week cleaning the house.

The problem is, Dave thinks that the cleaning standard his mom adopted for her household should be the criteria by which all others are judged. While his mom's high standards might have been all right for that household, it should not become the norm for his. Laurie is a neat person but she isn't fastidious about cleanliness. Besides, she works a full-time job and is actively involved in church and with her kids. At this point in her family's life, keeping the house immaculate just isn't that important to her. Dave needs to "leave" his opinion and expectation regarding perfect housework.

Study Question

What expectations might you have brought into marriage which could be hindering your "becoming one"?

_____

_____

_____

2. We must leave certain behaviors that we observed in our family of origin. The behaviors may have worked or not worked but must be left behind if we are to become one. Both Dave and Laurie had parents who avoided conflict; they simply escaped into their own activities. For Dave and Laurie to experience healing, they will need to leave this unhealthy behavior behind by learning to face the issues and share the truth in love (Ephesians 4:15).

Study Question

> What behavior patterns, either positive or painful, might you have brought into marriage with anticipation that "this is the way it should be!"?

---

3. We must no longer look to our family of origin to meet our needs that our spouse should meet. This is why Laurie spends an inordinate amount of time at her parents' house. We all have a need for attention and we particularly need our spouse to meet that need. On a regular basis, we need our partner to enter into our world and spend undivided time with us. Dave is neglecting Laurie's need for attention by working too much. But instead of confronting the issue and lovingly talking it out, Laurie is escaping to her family of origin where her need for attention is abundantly met. Her need is legitimate, she's just seeking to have it met in an unhealthy manner. There's nothing wrong with her parents helping meet certain needs, but they shouldn't be the primary source—that's reserved for her husband.

Study Question

> What needs might you still be looking to have met through your family of origin, thus hindering marital giving and oneness?

_____

_____

4. We must "leave" unresolved pain and damaged emotions from our past. When Laurie was twelve years old, her biological father had an extramarital affair. Within a year her parents divorced. Unfortunately, Laurie was caught in the middle of the entire situation. She heard the accusations, felt the anger, and saw the grief. She was hurt, embarrassed, and became suspicious and distrustful of men. Although Dave had proven himself to be a "one woman man," Laurie struggled with jealousy. Every time he worked late, went on a business trip, or talked to a woman on the phone, she would ask questions, insinuate accusations, and become emotionally unsettled. The only way for Laurie to become free from her inordinate jealousy is for her to "leave" the pain of her childhood. Consider again the concept of the emotional cup. (See Chapter 4.)

Study Question

What issues of hurt, anger, fear, condemnation, or guilt might you have brought into marriage from your growing up years?

_____

_____

John 8:32 states that, *"the truth will set you free."* Have you ever analyzed your marriage relationship, looking for areas in which you have not yet "left" your family of origin? Have you embraced the truth about the four issues mentioned above? As you journey together through the exercises that follow, be open to God's gentle work in your life as the Great Physician.

Biblical Perspective

THE MYSTERY OF LEAVING, CLEAVING, AND BECOMING ONE

A mong the very first teachings of Scripture is the command to leave father and mother in order to cleave as one in marriage. The apostle Paul referred to this command as "a profound mystery" and even used it to further explain the relationship between Christ and His church (Ephesians 5:31-32). The principles proclaimed in this verse are cloaked with mystery and for every married couple the mystery is both profound and practical. Inherent in the mystery of this verse is a timeless truth for God's three divinely ordained relationships—marriage, family, and the church.

> *"'For my thoughts are not your thoughts, neither are your ways My ways,' declares the Lord"* *(Isaiah 55:8).*

The Mystery of Divine Explanation— "For this Reason"

This divine commandment is preceded by Adam's momentous declaration in Genesis 2:23, *"this is now bone of my bone and flesh of my flesh."* It is for this cause, this reason, that a man should forsake all other intimate human relationships— for the inexpressible joy of committed companionship and the security of mutual love in marriage. As a part of what Elohim declared to be "very good," it is this relationship that prompts this principle of leaving father and mother.

But why prioritize the marriage relationship above the family relationship? Could it be that families will be no stronger and no more divinely-centered than the marital oneness upon which they are built? A healthy family must have as its foundation, a healthy marriage.

The marriage relationship portrayed the holy love affair between Christ and the Church even before there was a Church! God was concerned about our families before they existed and burdened for us to become a Bride to His Son long before His coming. The beauty and complexity of God's provision and foresight underscores the declaration of Isaiah 55:8, *"'For my thoughts are not your thoughts, neither are your ways My ways,' declares the Lord."*

Study Questions

In what ways is the marriage relationship intended to be a model of Christ's relationship with the church?

_____

_____

_____

How might this priority of marriage be a part of God's plan to build strong foundations for families? Churches? Communities?

_____

_____

_____

The Mystery of Divine Exhortation—"shall a man leave"

There is a divinely declared order here: leave, then cleave, then become one. The significance of this exhortation is reinforced by Jesus during His earthly ministry (Matthew 19:4-6, Mark 10:6-9), and by the apostle Paul (Ephesians 5:31).

To "leave" is to loosen oneself, to prioritize or forsake one relationship for another. It speaks of a certain exclusiveness and is exemplified in the Old Testament when Boaz blessed Ruth over her leaving father and mother to come *"to a people that you did not previously know"* (Ruth 2:11). The word is used to reassure Israel that Elohim would not fail them or *"forsake them"* (Deuteronomy 31:8).

This progressive and faith-filled journey of "leaving father and mother" will loosen one's soul to truly love and embrace another. The mind will forsake preconceived expectations and fantasies of how others, and particularly a spouse, must be. Our emotions will be freed from dependent, self-interested love, and the inevitable pain which occurs in a fallen world. Our will is allowed to embrace new behaviors which are right and true for the new marriage relationship. The inner longing for human intimacy will no longer be directed toward the family of origin but toward the new relationship of marriage.

To "cleave" is to be united, to cling together, and it communicates a priority of loyalty. The New Testament speaks of being "joined together" and that mere man should not seek to separate that which has been divinely united (Mark 10:9). This cleaving in marriage portrays the selfless devotion of committed love. What is the origin of such loving loyalty? It is part of this mystery that we must first cleave to the One who is love (1 John 4:16). *"And you have been given fullness in Christ . . . ."* (Colossians 2:10).

To "become one" in marriage is to enjoy a communion of spirit in the things of God, a community of friendship as soulmates and companions, and a consummation of sexual expression in committed love. It is to bring into unity two distinct creations of divine worth, God joining them together in spirit, soul, and body (Genesis 2:7).

Study Questions

What areas of "leaving" have you seen effectively working in your marriage?

_____

_____

_____

In what ways do you feel you and your spouse have effectively worked at "cleaving" together?

_____

_____

_____

During the course of this study, what have been some effective "becoming one" experiences?

_____

_____

_____

The Mystery of Divine Example

Paul's discussion of the mystery of Christ and the Church is closely related to this principle of leaving and cleaving. How is it that this verse on leaving, cleaving, and becoming one speaks to the mystery of Christ and the Church?

- Was it not Christ who left His Father? *"Regarding not equality with God as a thing to be grasped, but emptied Himself . . . becoming obedient to the point of death, even death on a cross"* (Philippians 2:6-8);

- In order that He might cleave to His bride, *"For we have become united with Him"* (Romans 6:5);

- So that we, with Him, might become one, *"But the one who joins himself to the Lord is one Spirit with Him"* (1 Corinthians 6:17).

The mystery of Genesis 2:24 is a profound key to marriage oneness. Many couples struggle for decades only to find themselves still dealing with unresolved issues surrounding this principle. God has not left us without instruction. Consider it. Explore it. Experience the truth of it!

Experiencing Biblical Truth

EXPLORE A BETTER UNDERSTANDING OF YOUR OWN NEEDS

You'll never be any more sensitive to the pain and needs of others than you are to your own! A self-reliant person, claiming to need very little, is most often not very sensitive to others' needs. If you live in denial about your own needs or pain, you may view others as selfish or overly needy. Exploring your own needs might include discussing the following questions with your spouse:

• Complete sentences like, "I feel loved by my spouse when

_____."

• Review a list of intimacy needs to see which three are most meaningful to you as an adult (see Chapter 2). How might the three you picked relate to your growing up?

• Consider which intimacy needs you might have missed to some significant degree during childhood, i.e., "I missed out on individual attention—time spent just with me doing things I enjoyed."

"I think I may have missed _____ from my father."

"I think I may have missed _____ from my mother."

Heal the Pain of Your Unmet Needs

Denial of your own pain will have its effect on your spouse, children, and others. Unresolved anger from the past might be displaced upon others. Seeking to minimize or explain away your hurt may keep you insensitive to your spouse's hurt, demanding that he or she respond as you have.

This healing process might include the following:

Review the four key intimacy needs listed below, indicating with an " **X** " needs you missed from both parents, a half-circle " **C** " for those your father met, an opposing half-circle " **Ɔ** " for those your mother met, and a full circle " **O** " for those both your mother and father met.

Attention—to take thought of another and convey appropriate interest, concern, and support; to enter into another's world

Approval—to accept as satisfactory; to give formal or official sanction to; to have and express a favorable opinion

Affection—to communicate care and closeness through physical touch and verbalized love

Comfort—to come alongside with word, feeling, and touch; to give consolation with tenderness

Take turns sharing with each other the hurt that you experienced as a result of these basic intimacy needs not being met in your growing up years. Practice comforting your spouse as the hurts are shared; allow your spouse to comfort you.

Examples:

- **Attention**—I really missed my father entering my world. *Spouse's response*: That really saddens me. It really hurts me to hear that; I love you so much.

- **Approval**—I never sensed or heard that anyone was proud of me. *Spouse's response*: I deeply regret your not having more approval; it hurts me that you missed it; I'm proud of you and I love you.

- **Affection**—I missed hearing verbalized love from my mother. *Spouse's response*: As I think of you growing up without hearing verbalized love, it just makes me so sad for you, and for how that must have felt.

- **Comfort**—When I experienced hurt and pain growing up, there was seldom anyone there to share my pain with; and when I was able to share my pain, I often just got advice instead of comfort. *Spouse's response*: I'm sad that you had to hurt alone. It's so important to be comforted when we're hurting—I'm sorry you missed that.

Begin renewing your mind by replacing lies with God's truth (God says I'm beloved, a saint, a joint-heir, etc.), and the truth that your spouse loves you! Focus on part of the "Divine Mystery of Marriage:"

- You are part of God's plan to restore to your spouse some of the unmet needs from his or her growing up years.

- No other person on planet Earth (6.5 billion people) has been called of God like you have for this divinely ordained role!

Praxis

CAN YOU IDENTIFY GENUINE LOVE?

A Project for a Marriage Staff Meeting and/or Family Night

Read together and discuss 1 Corinthians 13. Each of the questions below may have several good answers but select the most precise illustration to match the questions on love. Discuss how you see your spouse and then other family members demonstrating each one:

_____ 1. How can I show you that I am patient?

_____ 2. How can I show you special kindness?

_____ 3. How can I show you that I am not envious?

_____ 4. How can I show you that I am not trying to impress you?

_____ 5. How can I show you that I am not proud?

_____ 6. How can I show you that you are more important to me than I am to myself?

_____ 7. How can I show you that I am not defensive?

_____ 8. How can I show you that I have erased the memory of an offense?

_____ 9. How can I show you that I am not delighting in your defeats?

_____ 10. How can I show you that I am happy when you make difficult but right decisions?

A. By not reminding you of your past failures.

B. By being helpful to you during sickness and disappointment.

C. By understanding your struggle and praising your standard.

D. By not sharing your defeats with others.

E. By not getting irritated when you don't understand me.

F. By not reacting when you show me that I am wrong.

G. By making your personal needs a priority in my schedule.

H. By not promoting my own skills or accomplishments, but by praising the efforts of others.

I. By treating you as I would want myself to be treated.

J. By telling others how God is working through you.

CHAPTER EIGHT

Ministering With a Great Commandment Heart

Phil and Susy's Journey

It was midnight when Sal called. I immediately knew he was in trouble. "Phil, I need your help. I know you don't practice criminal law, but I need you to get me out of jail. Would you be willing to post bond for me? I don't have my wallet, but if you'll get me out of here, I'll cover you tomorrow when the banks open." Even in a crisis, Sal was calm and businesslike.

Sal was not a distant alcoholic uncle or an unstable homeless man. Sal was chairman of the board, CEO, COO, and CFO of a large company which annually gave ten percent of its profits to charity. Sal had been driving hard for thirty years, plowing his way to the top. Even as a new believer, he was very active for the Lord raising funds and charting the course for various Christian ministries. He also established a fund that enabled inner-city children to attend Christian camps.

It saddens me to admit that Sal was my disciple. I had spent over two hundred hours with him in my early years of discipling men, working through *Operation Timothy*. We studied topics like who Jesus is, how to receive His acceptance and forgiveness, how to gain assurance of eternal life, understanding the Holy Spirit, victory over temptation, and gaining a vision for being salt and light in our world. Sal and I discussed principles of studying the Bible, understanding the value of prayer, choosing a church, developing godly character, and discerning God's will and responding in obedience. We had even planned on studying the *Operation Timothy* material on more detailed issues such as ministering in the home and integrating Christian principles in the workplace.

But I never got to know the real Sal. Like a "connect the dots" game, I pushed him from point 1 to 2 to 3 along a prescribed study course; and like good, disciplined businessmen, we never deviated from the plan. But when Sal called that Sunday evening, I realized for the first time that I had failed him. Because I was never open and vulnerable with Sal, he didn't feel comfortable sharing with me his secret sin. In retrospect, I never revealed to Sal my challenges. I never confided in Sal that Susy and I had struggles in our marriage. Our sharing was surface, superficial, and professional. It broke my heart to realize that I had failed my friend, the Lord, and the discipleship process by selfishly protecting my own feelings and weaknesses. Because of my facade, Sal didn't sense that our relationship was a safe place in which he could vulnerably share.

I do remember Sal sharing with me some superficial remarks about having problems at home, but when the conversation drifted towards emotional issues, I promptly responded with a choice Bible verse. One of my pat answers was to quote Romans 8:28, "*And we know that in all things God works for the good of those who love Him, who have been called according to His purpose.*"

So when I first heard Sal's voice on the phone that night, I had no clue why he was in trouble. With my practical mind, I asked why Angie, his wife, couldn't vouch for him and post his bail. There must have been a mistake. His response stunned me. With a perfectly calm voice, Sal told me that Angie was in the hospital being treated for head wounds. In that shocking moment, I realized for the first time that I had been meeting weekly for over two years with a man who regularly beat his wife. Because of her love for Sal, Angie had always remained silent about the abuse. But this time Angie's bruised face could not heal in seclusion— she had been knocked unconscious when Sal slammed her against the fireplace hearth.

When Sal asked for my help, I did one of the hardest things I've ever done, and from time to time I still question my decision. Instead of coming to Sal's rescue, I chose not to bail him out of jail because I felt that God was dealing with both my dishonesty with Sal and his dishonesty with the Lord.

Eventually, Sal called his operations manager to help him. The incident didn't disrupt his business too much, but it devastated his home life.

After that Sunday night, Sal and I remained cordial, and we even saw each other from time to time. But he never wanted to meet with me again or talk about spiritual things. My calls to him were always cut short by a business meeting or call that he had to take. Several years later I read in the paper that Sal had been arraigned in a Superior Court for assault and battery. His secret sin was finally public.

Through my experience with Sal, I realized that discipleship requires both the sharing of spiritual truth and the impacting of life. The apostle Paul said it this way, *"We loved you so much that we were delighted to share with you not only the gospel of God but our lives as well, because you had become so dear to us"* (1 Thessalonians 2:8). To be effective, we must seek to fulfill the Great Commission (Matthew 28:19-20) with a Great Commandment heart (Matthew 22:37-39). In discipleship relationships, imparting truth is critical but not sufficient by itself. We must first love God and others with all our hearts. Only then will we be in a position to teach them truth.

David and Teresa's Reflections

It's amazing to think that Phil could have spent so much time with Sal and still not known of his critical marital problems. But to some degree, I'm sure we're guilty of emphasizing people's *knowledge* of Scripture so much that we ignore whether or not the Scriptures are genuinely impacting their lives. There's a significant difference between imparting truth and imparting life. For effective ministry, we really must do both, and the latter is more difficult and risky than the former. For relationships to flourish, they need the vulnerable sharing of one's life. Imparting life requires having a Great Commandment love toward others. It is a self-sacrificing, vulnerable type of love.

It's fascinating how people can "play the game" and act like everything's okay when it's not. Here's another story which illustrates the old adage, "You can't tell a book by its cover."

For 30 years Sam has faithfully attended his church. He's one of those "every time the doors are open" members.

His pastor is a renowned Bible expositor. Books, tapes, conferences, radio broadcasts—they are all a part of the trappings of his high-profile ministry. He is, in truth, a great teacher, "rightly dividing the word of truth" Sunday after Sunday.

Sam, one of 3,000 church members, has sat in the pew and has listened to his pastor preach at least twice a week, 52 weeks a year, for 30 years. Sam has heard a lot of sermons.

Sam also attends Sunday School. Along with 80 other adults, he sits in the same room Sunday after Sunday listening to a lecture. His teacher is an articulate spokesperson and has been teaching a survey course of the entire Bible for the past eight years. They're currently studying the book of Amos—in particular, the prediction of the dispersion and restoration of Israel and the impending judgments on surrounding nations.

While at church, Sam seems to be doing what's expected of a good church member. He's always there, he cordially (but superficially) relates to others, and he even tithes. But at home, Sam is skating on thin ice.

He and his wife have drifted into an unfulfilling, barely tolerable relationship. He brings home the bread and she bakes it, but that's about the extent of their "togetherness." They have both thought about divorce, even threatened a time or two, but know enough of the Bible to realize that divorce is not a good option. Several years ago, their pastor preached a sermon on Malachi 2:16. Though they did not discuss it, Sam and his wife eliminated divorce as a way to deal with the emptiness and pain of their relationship.

Sam is a desperate man, standing on shifting sand.

Sam's children tend to live their own lives. His lack of relational involvement has forced them to look elsewhere for many of their relational and emotional needs. Fortunately, his daughter has gravitated toward the church youth group. Unfortunately, his son has found companionship with a group of renegades at school. Sam has tried to set and enforce some "spiritual" rules with his children, but for some reason they're not responding.

Personally, Sam struggles. His anger constantly simmers just below the boiling point; periodically it erupts into outburst. He also struggles with fear, insecurity, and selfishness.

When Thoreau said, "Most men lead lives of quiet desperation," he could have been talking about Sam. When Jesus described a *"foolish man who built his house on sand,"* (Matthew 7:26) He was picturing Sam. Sam is a desperate man standing on shifting sand.

How can someone so religious be so miserable? How can someone who has heard so much biblical truth be so close to personal and family disaster?

While Sam may mentally know the truth, he is not experiencing it. He has memorized 1 John 4:18, but he's still fearful. He's heard sermons on marriage and family, but he doesn't live what he knows.

Who is at fault?

Ultimately, Sam must give an account of himself to God, so the issue stops with him. But secondarily, one has to question: a Christian education philosophy and system in which a student could hear Bible messages for thirty years and not demonstrate positive changes in lifestyle or improvements in interpersonal relationships; a system that correctly teaches "what" to believe; a system that doesn't provide relational accountability; a system that doesn't encourage relational involvement and intimacy.

Who is at fault?

Romans 14:12 and James 3:11 issue the verdict.

"Restoring a Great Commandment Heart"

It was Passion week and almost a year of opposition from the religious leaders was about to climax at the cross. Throughout the week, Jesus would spend time at the temple during the day and return to Bethany at night. Perhaps He stayed in the home of His beloved friends Martha, Mary, and Lazarus. Jesus experienced ever increasing opposition in the daylight hours and the caring love of disciples and friends at night. On one day trip, Jesus could no longer tolerate the religious apathy and hypocrisy He saw at the temple and He, *"began driving out those who were buying and selling. He overturned the tables of the money changers and the benches of those selling doves . . . and said 'Is it not written: My house will be called a house of prayer for all nations?'"* (Mark 11:15-17). As a result, the Scriptures say that, *"the chief priests and teachers of the law began looking for a way to kill Him"* (Mark 11:18).

On another day, recorded in Mark 11:27, the religious leaders, one group at a time, challenged Jesus, trying to trap Him. First, it was the chief priests, scribes, and elders who came asking, *"By what authority are you doing these things?"* (Mark 11:28) Then the Pharisees and Herodians challenged Jesus by asking: *"Is it right to pay taxes to Caesar or not?"* (Mark 12:14) And finally the Sadducees, who didn't believe there was a resurrection, invented a story of seven brothers who married the same woman and asked, *"at the resurrection whose wife will she be?"* (Mark 12:23) Each time, Jesus deftly sent his challengers away amazed and confounded.

Into that "stump the teacher" atmosphere, a lone scribe appeared. (Scribes were experts in the law.) The scribe had heard the debating and had seen how well Jesus had answered the religious leaders. During a lull in the debate, he stepped up and posed a question to Jesus, asking, *"Of all the commandments, which is the most important?"* (Mark 12:28) Was his question a sincere one? Was he, like the others, trying to "trap the teacher" in His words? Did he just love theological debate? We don't know, but his question was a good one. Jewish rabbis counted 613 individual statutes of the law and constantly tried to differentiate which were "heavy" and which were "light"— which were the most important and which were not as important.

Without hesitation, Jesus answered, *"The most important one is this: 'Hear, O Israel, the Lord our God is one. Love the Lord your God with all your heart and with all your soul and with all your mind and with all your strength.' The second is this: 'Love your neighbor as yourself.'" There is no other commandment greater than these"* (Mark 12:29-31).

Where did Jesus find these commandments? Where did they appear originally? The first part of Jesus' answer came from Deuteronomy 6:4-6, verses that are known as the "shema," the Hebrew word for "hear." Even today the "shema" is the call to worship in synagogue services. Two thoughts are intriguing: Why did Jesus bypass the "big ten," the Ten Commandments given in the book of Exodus? Weren't the Ten Commandments the very core of the law and God's first written communication to His people Israel after they had come out of bondage in Egypt? Secondly, the setting for the book of Deuteronomy provides an interesting insight. Deuteronomy is a sermon to a completely different generation of people than those who came out of Egypt and who had received the Ten Commandments. Because of the people's disobedience, God caused them to wander in the wilderness for 40 years—long enough for all but two, Joshua and Caleb, to die. Deuteronomy was spoken by Moses to those born wandering in the wilderness. Was God stressing to this second generation what their parents had forgotten?

> *Why did Jesus bypass the "big ten," the Ten Commandments given in the book of Exodus?*

The second part of Jesus' answer came from the book of Leviticus, a book written to the first generation that came out of Egypt. What's interesting about this aspect of the "great commandment" is its location—Leviticus 19:18: *"Do not seek revenge or bear a grudge against one of your people, but love your neighbor as yourself."* If "X" generally marks the spot for treasure, who would have thought that treasure was buried in Leviticus 19? Why did Jesus find treasure in this particular verse? Why did Jesus pull together two commandments spoken in two different generations and call them the "Great Commandment?"

A Message to Empower the Church

It's the Great Commandment heart which empowered the first century church. To read the first chapters of Acts, it is clear that they were loving God with all that they were, and were loving their neighbors as themselves:

> *"They devoted themselves to the apostles' teaching and to the fellowship, to the breaking of bread and to prayer.*

Everyone was filled with awe, and many wonders and miraculous signs were done by the apostles. All the believers were together and had everything in common. Selling their possessions and goods, they gave to anyone as he had need. Every day they continued to meet together in the temple courts. They broke bread in their homes and ate together with glad and sincere hearts, praising God and enjoying the favor of all the people. And the Lord added to their number daily those who were being saved" (Acts 2:42-47).

We find similar encouragement from the Epistles. Romans 13:9-10 restates the fact that every other commandment may be summed up in one rule: *"Love your neighbor as yourself . . . and love is the fulfillment of the law."* Other verses similarly focus in on love: Hebrews 13:1, Galatians 5:13, and 1 Corinthians 13. John's burdened appeal to the church at Ephesus states that they had left their first love (Revelation 2:4). And in the light of Matthew's end time prediction *"because of the increase in wickedness, the love of many will grow cold"* (Matthew 24:12), the challenge to minister from a Great Commandment heart may represent, for God's people, the great crisis—and opportunity—of the 21st century church.

Ingredients of a Great Commandment Heart

A Great Commandment heart pursues intimacy with God and with others. Significantly, Christ's great commandment spoke both of a vertical relationship with God and a horizontal relationship with others. Two commandments became the "Great Commandment" because the two are inextricably related. John wrote, *"If anyone says, 'I love God,' yet hates his brother, he is a liar. For anyone who does not love his brother, whom he has seen, cannot love God, whom he has not seen"* (1 John 4:20). Jesus taught this in the parable of the Good Samaritan. Enjoying eternal life involves "loving God" and "loving your neighbor," and Jesus taught that a neighbor is anyone in need.

How does a Great Commandment heart pursue intimacy with God and others? *Intimacy is pursued through relational experience based on truth.* Significantly, Christ's Great Commandment spoke of relationships and not rules. Why not just focus on keeping the Ten Commandments and the other rules? Christ's answer seems to say, "if you truly love the One behind the rules, then everything else will follow. It's My compelling love that empowers righteous living." Christ's earthly ministry models for us what loving others looks like. His focus was on relating to others in love, not merely keeping external rules. When challenged by the Pharisees about why His disciples were picking grain on the Sabbath (working), Jesus responded that *"the Sabbath was made for man, not man for the Sabbath"* (Mark 2:27). Compassion for people was to be at the heart of true religion. When we focus on external rules, internal love is quenched. Empowered by His Spirit and equipped by His Word, the church becomes equipped to experience love with God and others.

And why does a Great Commandment heart pursue intimacy with God and others? Because God has made provision for both our aloneness and our fallenness. Only love satisfies both human dilemmas. It is love, portrayed at Calvary, that satisfies the penalty for our sin; and it's the God who *is* love who makes provision for our sin so that we can lovingly relate to Him, removing our aloneness. It's as if Christ would say to the scribe, "It's love that satisfies all other rules."

"We love because He first loved us" (1 John 4:19). There is no greater demonstration of this provision for aloneness and fallenness than to explore the question—where does the love come from that we might love God and others? The love comes from God! Just stop and imagine: we have a God who gives us the Great Commandment and then gives us His love to fulfill it!

Experiencing Great Commandment Love in Marriage

So how does this relate to marriage? Could it be that marriage is part of God's plan for you and me to learn to love just one person, and then a few others called children (family), and then a few more through our witness and through discipleship? Perhaps marriage is a laboratory in which we can learn to live selflessly and vulnerably with others. Perhaps it is in marriage that we experience a true "imparting of our life" to another person. Maybe it is in the marriage relationship that we can learn to experience confession, forgiveness, comfort, and speaking the truth in love.

It is our hope that these marriage principles have been an encouragement to your marriage and that they will help equip you to fulfill the Great Commission with a Great Commandment love.

Biblical Perspective

GRACE: ENABLING INTIMACY

Intimacy has been described as genuinely knowing another person, and becoming caringly involved in their life as we allow them to know us in a similar way. Additionally, we can identify various "intimacy needs" such as acceptance, attention, affection, appreciation, and comfort. But there must be a "power" outside ourselves that enables us to genuinely experience intimacy.

The complexity and overwhelming "neediness" of our human condition means that relationships tend to move toward deterioration. It's what happens when two humanly bankrupt partners join forces together in marriage. It is what has been described as each partner becoming like a tick on a dog—"I'm here to take from you"—only to discover in such a marriage that there are two ticks and no dog! Our only hope is outside ourselves. An unlimited source of love, acceptance, comfort, and forgiveness is needed to enable and sustain an intimate relationship. Such a source is available, and His name is Jesus. The Bible calls this divine contribution—grace!

> " *. . . as good stewards of the manifold grace of God"*
> *(1 Peter 4:10, NASB).*

Grace Initiates

Divine grace initiates our intimate relationship with God. It was Christ who humbled Himself, took on the form of a servant, and became obedient to the point of death (Philippians 2:7-10) . . . that we might become partakers in the divine nature (2 Peter

1:4).   Noted Bible scholar Donald Barnhouse speaks of our undeserved gift of grace in this way: "love that goes upward is worship; love that goes outward is affection; love that stoops is grace."   Christ "stooped" from heaven, entered into my world, and gave *Himself*.   What an example!   Having partaken of this divine initiative, a spouse is enabled to initiate caring involvement in a partner's life.   It is this initiative that genuinely communicates, "I was thinking of you," and "I care."

Grace Liberates

> *I'm now free to look beyond others' faults and see their needs.*

It is also grace that frees us from the penalty of sin and grants us eternal life so that one day we will be free from the presence of sin (Titus 3:5-7).   But much more than this, it is grace that can liberate us from the power of sin in this life.

- There's liberty from selfishness . . . freeing me to see and give to the needs of others.

- There's liberty from criticism . . . freeing me from judging others.

Just as Christ looked beyond my faults and saw my needs, I am now also free to look beyond others' faults and see their needs.   Instead of judging another's behavior, we now have the freedom to give unselfishly in meeting their intimacy needs (Philippians 2:3).

Study Question

List areas of personal liberty that you've experienced during this study.

_____

_____

Grace Motivates

Living in the awe and wonder of all that we have and are in Christ motivates a stewardship of grace.

This life of intimacy with God and others is not lived out in obligation or duty. There wells up within believers such a joyful gratefulness and humble appreciation that giving unconditionally to a spouse, child, friend, or even to our enemy is uncontrollable! Out of our innermost being will flow rivers of living water that nourish intimacy in human relationships (John 7:38). Grace is infectious, contagious—the love of Christ is now "constraining" us (2 Corinthians 5:14).

Study Question

List areas of giving and loving in your marriage in which you have experienced additional motivation during this study.

_____

_____

_____

_____

Grace Lubricates

Charles Swindoll, in *The Grace Awakening*, speaks of the marriage "oiled by grace." It's grace that lubricates the inevitable rough edges of our humanness. The demands and closeness of marriage and family inevitably bring the human rough spots to the surface—but the intimate relationship ministers the oil of God's grace:

• As acceptance is granted—in spite of "performance" (Romans 15:7)

- As edifying words are shared to build-up and encourage (Ephesians 4:29)

- As personal responsibility is emphasized in focusing on our walk with our Savior (Romans 14:10-12)

As we experience God's grace in relationships, we come to enjoy more abundance, the kind that exceeds anything we could ask for or think of (John 10:10, Ephesians 3:20).

Study Question

What other blessings of abundance have you experienced during this study with your spouse?

_____

_____

_____

_____

_____

_____

It's grace that lubricates the inevitable rough edges of our humanness.

Experiencing Biblical Truth

JOURNAL OF GRATEFULNESS— PSALM 103:2

"Forget None of His Benefits"

The Benefits of Gratefulness

Multiplied blessings are ours as we pause to *"forget none of His benefits"* toward us (Psalm 103:2). Among the numerous benefits of a grateful heart are the following:

- Gratefulness guards us from a critical, negative attitude.
- Gratefulness guards us from a judgmental spirit.
- Gratefulness, when expressed to others, can motivate them to continue in good deeds.
- Gratefulness, when acknowledged to God, is an important element of worship.

The Search for Blessings

Take time this week to identify blessings you've experienced during this study. Consider how you've been blessed through your spouse and/or other group members.

Additionally, you might regularly involve family members in a "blessing search" as each member shares a recent blessing and assumes responsibility for expressing appreciation. Where to look:

- Loved ones of whom you've recently been reminded in a special way

- Character qualities in your spouse, family, or friends which are inspiring to you

- Often over-looked blessings of life, health, provision, and creation

- Specific answers to prayer

- Spiritual realities such as our salvation, the Scriptures, and God's Holy Spirit, grace, and comfort

The Expression of Appreciation

Appreciation helps seal in our hearts the reality of our blessings, and when we express appreciation, others are blessed and encouraged. Appreciation can be shared:

- Verbally, with a simple "thanks"

- In writing, with a note of appreciation

- Publicly, as testimony is given of our genuine gratitude

Our verbal thanks and testimony to others are of major importance.

How We have Been Blessed

Look for God's interventions, expressions of family member love, answered prayers, and special people, events, and experiences that have impacted our lives.

How We Share Our Appreciation

Say "Thanks," write a note, give a gift, give testimony.

Partnership Follow-Up Plan

To help keep your "Unlimited Partnership" healthy, consider completing the following list of "intimate encounters." To help you better identify the type of intimate encounters you and your spouse enjoy, check the items you think would most appeal to your mate and then check the items you would most enjoy. Then compare lists and design a follow-up plan to address the ones you agree to pursue.

Mate	Myself	
❏	❏	Holding hands
❏	❏	Going for a walk
❏	❏	Receiving an unexpected hug
❏	❏	Finding a love note
❏	❏	Receiving a surprise gift
❏	❏	Being served a favorite meal
❏	❏	Being told "I love you"
❏	❏	Helping with the kids
❏	❏	Being approached sexually
❏	❏	Seeing an orderly house
❏	❏	Seeing the lawn looking nice
❏	❏	Receiving a compliment on appearance
❏	❏	Taking a shower together
❏	❏	Going on a surprise date
❏	❏	Getting a back rub or massage
❏	❏	Having dinner out
❏	❏	Being praised for achievements
❏	❏	Having a quiet conversation

Praxis

MARRIAGE STAFF MEETING DISCUSSION QUESTIONS

The next time you have a Marriage Staff Meeting, feel free to use the guide provided below as a catalyst for good, productive conversation:

1. If I were to describe my marriage after this study with one word, the word I would use would be _____.

2. What words do you think your spouse would use to describe your marriage?

3. What benefits are you receiving from your marriage relationship that you wouldn't be receiving if you had remained single? Be specific.

4. What strengths have you discerned in your spouse during this study? How will you express your awareness?

5. During this study, what has your spouse done that made you feel particularly loved or valued?

6. What do you plan to do to better express your love and appreciation toward your spouse?

7. What additional efforts toward intimacy have you seen your spouse make? How have you expressed gratefulness for these efforts?

8. What are some of your present goals for your marriage? What can you do differently that will enable you both to reach them?

Here are some suggestions on what answers to number 8 might look like:

- I will show more of an interest in my spouse's activities by asking questions.

- I will spend more time thinking about positive factors in my marriage relationship and attempting to discover ways to be what my spouse wants and needs.

- I will take time to pray for and with my family, especially my spouse.

- If I have any resentments against family members—particularly my spouse—I will forgive them now.

APPENDIX A

Steps to Peace with God

As we have shared our stories and the truths we have learned through the pages of this book, it has not been our desire to commend ourselves, but to assure you that there is hope. Your troubled marriage—or that of someone dear to your heart—can be salvaged and transformed! But you can't do it on your own. Even if you don't have to deal with deep-seated anger or anxiety, many tensions exist in modern-day life which impact each of us. High divorce rates, workplace pressures, and the fracturing of extended families in our society can serve to undermine even the healthiest union of husband and wife.

We are convinced that the beginning of healing and restoration in marriage is found in a personal relationship with Jesus Christ. As He said about Himself, *"I am the way, and the truth, and the life; no one comes to the Father, but through Me"* (John 14:6). He not only shows us the way to heaven, but how to enjoy the "abundant life" that He promised to His children (John 10:10).

At this point in your life, if you have not responded to Christ, accepting His free gift of salvation and eternal life, there is no better time to do so than right now. How? The following are some simple, straightforward guidelines called, "Steps to Peace with God." Please read through them slowly and carefully. At the end is a suggested prayer which you can use, or you can just pray in your own words. The important thing is to acknowledge your need of Him and ask the Lord to take control of your life. More than anything else, this is what began the work of transformation in our lives that has utterly healed our marriages.

Steps to Peace with God

Step 1: God's Purpose: Peace and Life.

God loves you and wants you to experience peace and life— abundant and eternal.

The Bible says:

". . . *We have peace with God through our Lord Jesus Christ"* (Romans 5:1).

"For God so loved the world, that He gave His only begotten Son, that whoever believes in Him should not perish, but have eternal life" (John 3:16).

"The thief comes only to steal, and kill, and destroy; I came that they might have life, and might have it abundantly" (John 10:10).

Since God planned for us to have peace and abundant life right now, why are most people not having this experience?

Step 2: Our Problem—Separation.

God created us in HIS own image to have an abundant life. But we have chosen instead to live for ourselves. We have disobeyed God and gone our own willful way. We still make this choice today. This results in separation from God.

The Bible says:

"For all have sinned and fall short of the glory of God" (Romans 3:23).

"For the wages of sin is death [separation from God], but the free gift of God is eternal life in Christ Jesus our Lord" (Romans 6:23).

In other words, our rebellion results in separation from God.

Our attempts: Through the ages, individuals have tried in many ways to bridge this gap, without success.

But the Bible says: *"There is a way which seems right to a man, but its end is the way of death"* (Proverbs 14:12).

The reason why man's efforts fail to bridge the gap is found in the Bible: *"For by grace you have been saved through faith; and that not of yourselves, it is the gift of God; not as a result of works, that no one should boast"* (Ephesians 2:8-9).

There is only one remedy for this problem of separation.

Step 3: God's Remedy—the Cross.

Jesus Christ is the ONLY answer to this problem. He DIED on the cross and ROSE from the grave, paying the penalty for our sin and bridging the gap between God and man.

The Bible says:

"For there is one God, and one mediator also between God and men, the man Christ Jesus" (1 Timothy 2:5).

"But God demonstrates His own love toward us, in that while we were yet sinners, Christ died for us" (Romans 5:8).

"Jesus said to him, "I am the way, and the truth, and the life; no one comes to the Father, but through Me" (John 14:6).

God has provided the ONLY way. . .we must make the choice.

Step 4: Our Response—Receive Christ.

We must TRUST JESUS CHRIST and RECEIVE HIM by personal invitation.

The Bible says:

"But as many as received Him, to them He gave the right to become children of God, even to those who believe in His name" (John 1:12).

". . . If you confess with your mouth Jesus as Lord, and believe in your heart that God raised Him from the dead, you shall be saved; for with the heart man believes, resulting in righteousness, and with the mouth he confesses, resulting in salvation" (Romans 10:9-10).

The question is, are you going man's way, meaning that you're trapped in sin, rebellion, separation from God, frustration, guilt, and lack of purpose? Or have you crossed the bridge with Christ, meaning that you know God and His peace, forgiveness, and abundant and eternal life?

Is there any reason why you cannot receive Jesus Christ right now? Here are the steps:

1. Admit your need. (**I am a sinner.**)

2. Turn from your sin. (**Repent.**)

3. Believe that Jesus Christ died for you on the cross and rose from the grave.

4. Through prayer, invite Jesus Christ to come in and control your life through the Holy Spirit. (**Receive Him as Lord and Savior.**)

Prayer is more than saying words. It is the attitude of your heart. If you desire to receive Christ, pray a prayer like the one on the following page:

WHAT TO PRAY:

Dear Lord Jesus,

I know that I am a sinner and need Your forgiveness. I believe that You died for my sins. I want to turn from my sins. I now invite You to come into my heart and life. I trust You as my Lord and Savior.

If you prayed this prayer, this is just the beginning of a wonderful new life in Christ! To deepen this relationship you should:

Read your Bible every day to get to know Christ better.

Talk to God in prayer every day.

Seek fellowship with other Christians so you can grow in Christ together.

Tell others about Christ.

Worship, fellowship, and serve with other Christians in a church where the Bible is preached.

As Christ's representative in a needy world, demonstrate your new life by your love and concern for others.

May God bless you as you do.

(Adapted from a booklet published by the Billy Graham Evangelistic Association. Scripture quotations are taken from the New American Standard Bible. Reprinted with permission.)

Following Up

If you have just prayed the prayer at the end of "Steps to Peace with God," or are renewing a commitment to God that you have made in the past, the Discipleship Network of America and

Intimate Life Ministries offer a variety of resources that can help you get off to a strong start in your relationship with God. We also offer resources to help improve your marriage and family life.

Coming to Christ is beginning the most wonderful journey in the world, and in fact, eternity! And the greatest need for each of us who have made this decision is the need to be discipled— that is, finding a spiritual parent (2 Timothy 2:2). For more information concerning how you can begin a discipleship relationship, please see *Eternal Impact* in the resource section.

APPENDIX B

A Note from Phil & Susy

It is our privilege to serve you and the Lord in our common desire to be more Christ-like in marriage, family, church, work, and reaching others in a gentle and yet bold way with the love of Jesus Christ. God has called us to do this through Discipleship Network of America, a network of people committed to reaching and discipling others—serving pastors; church, denominational and parachurch leaders; men's ministries; the homeschool community; and individuals ministering in their homes and at work.

In all of our books, whether the focus is couples, men, family, or church, we address practical, everyday needs, challenges, and pain with biblical answers. Because we have lived out His ministry first as a husband and wife and then as parents, our marriage and family have not only been the crucible for life change, but also the medium through which we transparently share life's joys, tears, failures, blessings, and eternally significant relationships in a way that we trust will encourage, equip, and release you to be more completely one of His precious life-changing disciples.

We are available to share through live conferences, retreats, church services, and seminars, in addition to doing outreaches to the uncommitted. We have also captured much of this live material in various video and audio series presented either individually, as a couple, or with our children, who also share transparently the journey of our family.

Please consider us the friends next door or down the street who may be of some help or encouragement to you, your marriage, family, church, ministry, or work, as you answer God's call to see your life as a channel of His life-changing love and forgiveness in building disciples.

APPENDIX C

About Phil & Susy

Phil Downer serves as President of Discipleship Network of America. DNA is a nationwide network of people committed to following Christ's example of winning and discipling others to become disciple makers. The spiritual reproductive ministry of DNA flows out of the lives of people focused on Christ in their work, marriage, family, neighborhood, and church.

Phil is a popular speaker at men's events, at couples' events with his wife of 35 years, Susy, and at family conferences with his children. He and Susy coauthored *Optimize Your Marriage: Making an Eternal Impact on Family and Friends*, which was released in July of 2003. He is also the author of *Eternal Impact: Investing in the Lives of Others, A Father's Reward: Raising Your Children to Walk in the Truth,* and *Brave, Strong, and Tender*— a book that details how this Viet Nam veteran learned to transfer his leadership from the battlefield to his home, his law practice, and eventually to a nationwide ministry. Phil is also the author of *Just an Ordinary Man* and editor and coauthor of *Effective Men's Ministry.*

A former machine gunner who served in Viet Nam with the United States Marine Corps in 1967-68, Phil received a Bachelor of Business Administration from Southern Methodist University in 1972 and a Juris Doctor from Emory University

School of Law in 1975. Phil was a successful lawyer before being led to Christ and discipled by fellow professionals. After leaving his position as a senior partner and member of the management team of a 50-attorney law firm, with offices in Atlanta, Washington, D.C., Dallas, and San Diego, he served as President of CBMC for a decade. Phil is on the Steering Committee of the National Coalition of Men's Ministries and is a past elder of his church and a member of CBMC.

Susy, also an attorney, graduated from SMU and Emory Law School and then served as Assistant Corporate Secretary and legal counsel for Delta Air Lines for ten years. She resigned her position with Delta in 1985 in order to devote herself full-time to their children, whom she has homeschooled throughout their education.

Phil and Susy have six children. Abigail, twenty-six, graduated from Covenant College, passed the CPA exam, and is now attending University of Tennessee Law School. Paul, twenty-four, graduated from Bryan College with degrees in both Business and Bible, and has joined the ministry of DNA. Matthew, twenty-two, is a senior at Harvard College. The twins, Anna and Joshua, twenty, are sophomores in college, at Bryan and Harvard, respectively. Susanna, fourteen, is still being educated at home.

APPENDIX D

Discipleship Network of America

Books by Phil Downer

Eternal Impact: Investing in the Lives of Others

In this powerful book, Phil details how we can leave a legacy that will endure forever through the lasting fruit of spiritual reproducers. This book offers men and women a realistic, step-by-step guide for building into and equipping people to become change agents in the world around them through discipleship. It includes instruction in finding a mentor and someone to disciple, living out your faith in the workplace and home, and learning to multiply your life by investing in the lives of others. Published in 1997 by Harvest House, the book has been endorsed by, among others, Dr. Joseph Stowell, former President of Moody Bible Institute; Jim Peterson, author of *Evangelism as a Lifestyle;* Ron Blue, President of Christian Financial Professionals Network; Kay Arthur, Executive Director of Precept Ministries; Howard Hendricks, Distinguished Professor, Dallas Theological Seminary; and Dr. Glenn Wagner, pastor and former Vice President of Promise Keepers. Its second edition was published by Eternal Impact Publishing in 2004. Each chapter includes questions for one-on-one or small group discussions.

A Father's Reward: Raising Your Children to Walk in the Truth

As a father of six, Phil understands the challenge of raising godly children in an ungodly world. In this book he addresses such topics as how to build loving relationships with children, create great family memories, help children find God's wisdom in everyday situations, discipline children biblically, conduct fun and effective family devotions, and prepare children to impact their world for Christ. Endorsers include Kay Arthur, Neil Anderson of Freedom in Christ Ministries, Steve Farrar, author and Director of Men's Leadership Ministries, Ron Blue, Steve Brown of Key Life Network, and Howard Hendricks. It was first published by Harvest House in 1998. Its second edition was published by Eternal Impact Publishing in 2005. Each chapter includes questions for one-on-one or small group discussions.

Brave, Strong, and Tender, in Everyday Spiritual Battles

Like it or not, men today are in a war—and the stakes are eternal. These are times that demand courage, strength, and tenderness. In this book, Phil addresses how men can gain victory God's way over an undisciplined faith, fleshly attitudes, and the challenges of life. Focusing on how to be a man of courage and a loving leader, husband, and father while developing an attitude of self-control and gentleness, this book will equip every man who reads it for transformative life change. Phil also addresses how to establish relationships of accountability, maintain commitments, and understand God's desire to work through our family, work, church, and life. First published in 1996 by Multnomah Books, this book has been endorsed by, among others, Bruce Wilkinson, founder of Walk Thru the Bible Ministries; Bill Armstrong, former United States Senator; Howard Hendricks; Patrick Morley, President of Man in the Mirror Ministries and author of *Man in the Mirror;* and Dr. Glenn Wagner. Its second edition was published by Eternal Impact Publishing in 2004. Each chapter includes questions for one-on-one or small group discussions.

Effective Men's Ministries: The Indispensable Toolkit For Your Church

Phil wrote two chapters and served as general editor of this book, which addresses how to develop a thriving men's ministry individually and in your church. This comprehensive handbook takes readers through the five stages of building a powerful, life-changing men's ministry. Some of the topics include teaching men to pray, becoming a spiritual parent, encouraging vital relationships, building unity in diversity, becoming irresistible husbands, and holding successful men's retreats. This book is endorsed by the National Coalition of Men's Ministries and includes twenty-five well-known authors some of whom are Ed Cole, Rod Cooper, Steve Farrar, Jack Hayford, and Steve Sonderman, with a foreword by Pat Morley. It was published by Zondervan in 2002.

Just An Ordinary Man

Do you ever feel ordinary, inadequate, or unappreciated? At one time or another, we all do. But these are exactly the moments in which God wants to intervene by empowering and equipping us to become His representatives. From great struggles emerge great leaders. Phil describes the principles of godly leadership through the life of Gene Ast, who struggled with a difficult childhood, low self-esteem, and poor reading and writing skills. Yet, because of his relationship with God, this ordinary man extraordinarily changed his world. This book was released in 2003 by Eternal Impact Publishing.

Books by Phil & Susy Downer

Unlimited Partnership: Building Intimacy & Teamwork Into Your Marriage

Coauthored by Phil and Susy with David and Teresa Ferguson, published in 1998 by Intimacy Press, and republished in 2007 by Eternal Impact Publishing, this is a practical resource aimed at enriching marital relationships. The authors open up their lives, marital struggles, problems, failures, and pain to provide a resource for building a more joyful, intimate, and cherishing marriage. This book offers insights into such issues as constructive ways of overcoming emotional distance and poor communication, the various aspects of true intimacy, guarding marriages from affairs, establishing emotional closeness, and identifying and overcoming baggage from your family of origin.

Optimize Your Marriage: Making an Eternal Impact on Family and Friends

Phil and Susy Downer share from their hearts and lives on creating a more joyful and intimate marriage and a lasting heritage of building Christ into your children. This book, released in 2003 by Christian Publications, includes a first-hand account of how God helped them overcome the selfishness, anger, and poor communication that nearly drove them to divorce court. Delve into *Optimize Your Marriage* for help in rebuilding relationships, overcoming past pain, operating your home in a loving and strategic way, finding the cornerstones of effective communication, building a dynamic family team, and effectively reaching others for Christ. Among its endorsers are Patrick Morley; Howard Hendricks; Bill Armstrong; Dr. Bob Horner, Senior Pastor, Peachtree Corners Baptist Church; Don Mitchell, former executive with General Motors and Chairman of the Board of CBMC International, and his wife, Nina; and Chris Van Brocklin, National Director of Men's Ministry, Evangelical Free Church of America.

All books can be ordered at www.DNAministries.org.

DNA Conferences & Retreats

Have you been thinking of having a men's, couples, or family conference, retreat, or outreach event for your church or community? Phil and his son, Paul, travel around the country full-time as a father-son speaking team, dynamically, vulnerably, and biblically addressing the most vital issues we face every day. For more details and available dates, check out our website (www.DNAministries.org) or call Phil (423.886.6362) to discuss scheduling a speaking engagement, outreach event, or one of DNA's six dynamic conferences described below.

Eternal Impact Conference

The Eternal Impact Weekend is a life-changing conference or retreat for men or couples which addresses the biblical principles of discipleship. Phil and Paul cover such topics as purity, healing brokenness, forgiving past sins, building intimacy into your marriage, investing your life in the life of a disciple, steps to strong relationships with your children, and overcoming the stumbling blocks to discipling others inside and outside your family.

- From Hell To Eternity Through Discipleship
- Oneness & Intimacy in Marriage Through Discipleship
- Leaving a Godly Legacy—Discipling Your Children
- Winning the Battle for Sexual Integrity
- Going Into the World & Making Disciples

Unlimited Partnership Conference

This weekend conference begins with the story of how Phil's anger, selfishness, driven work style, and infidelity almost destroyed Phil and Susy's marriage—until God restored it. Then, through powerful and practical teaching from the Word,

Phil teaches the keys to how every marriage can be built up and strengthened through the power of forgiveness, better communication skills, new habits of teamwork, and a renewed focus on intimacy in your marriage. This retreat or conference is designed for couples with a good marriage who would like to have an excellent marriage, for those who have a good marriage and would like a truly intimate partnership, and for those who have a broken marriage and need restoration.

- Marriages Can Thrive—Not Just Survive

- Intimacy & Communication

- Rebuilding Relationships, Healing Hurts, Restoring Trust

- Winning the Battle for Sexual Integrity (For Men Only); Marriage & Sexuality (For Women Only)

- The Marriage that Leaves an Eternal Legacy

Brave, Strong, & Tender Conference

This is a no-holds-barred retreat or conferences for every man ages 13 to 103! Drawing on the struggles of a difficult childhood, his combat experiences as a Marine machine gunner in Viet Nam, and the lessons he learned as he rose to become a managing partner of a 50 attorney law firm, Phil not only teaches but models God's ways of overcoming our past struggles and becoming God's soldiers in the battle for our families, businesses, churches, and communities. Presented by Phil and Paul as a father-son speaking team, this conference is strongly rooted in Scripture and addresses the keys to engaging and overcoming the challenging issues of anger, lust, apathy, a lack of discipline, and a spiritual coolness toward Christ. Every man who attends will be practically equipped and encouraged to follow our Lord and His Word in transformative ways in his relationships at home, work, and church.

- Gaining Victory Over an Undisciplined Faith, Attitude, and Life

- Developing the Biblical Disciplines of a One-Woman Man

- Succeeding in Accountability in a David & Jonathan Relationship

- Secrets of the Source: The Nonnegotiable Disciplines for Fruitfulness

- The Call To Battle!

A Father's Reward Conference

In this weekend retreat or conference, Phil and Paul explore the challenges of building close relationships, open communication, fun touch-points for family relationships, accountability, and character in raising children and grandchildren. It focuses on the goal of not merely raising children to be adults, but to be trained soldiers of the faith who are equipped to be disciple makers and world changers. An attempt is made to avoid only listing do's and don'ts which can sometimes just produce guilt. Rather, the emphasis is on God's grace, His principles, and how He wants to work, not only though our strengths, but also our weaknesses and failures, to teach our children how to "do life as Christians."

- The Results of the Teenage Years Without Godly Training

- Building Relationships with Peers and Parents

- Solving Conflicts Through Truth and Love

- Sexuality to Accountability: Ages eight to eighteen

- Reaching the Quarterlifer: Ages eighteen to twenty-eight

- Family Ministry That Is Fun and Fruitful

- Giving Your Children a Vision To Change the World

Family Conference

This conference is specially tailored to address the most critical issues facing the family today packaged in a format that is vulnerable, practical, and easily transferable into your everyday life. Phil and Paul (others of the Downers may also be available) share from their real-life struggles and experiences the biblical lessons God has taught them in areas of character development, conflict resolution, building relationships, overcoming destructive habits, dealing with the roots of bad attitudes, and gaining a vision to reach out to and impact those God has placed in your lives.

- As Parents, We are Watchmen for Our Family, Community, and Generation

- The Keys to Godly Discipline

- Teaching Your Children to Love God's Word

- Teaching Your Children to Work with Godly Diligence

- Resolving Conflicts through Truth and Love

- Purity and Accountability for Men, Young and Old

- Reaching and Discipling Others For Christ

A Leader After God's Own Heart Conference

This conference chronicles the life of Gene Ast who destroyed his reputation and nearly himself before learning to live out twelve leadership principles that transformed his whole life. Having come from a poor background, Gene became a mulit-millionaire through the development, design, and manufacture of a machine that revolutionized an entire industry in the northwestern part of the United States. This is a study of the life of a man and the life truths he discovered that are grounded in Scripture and vitally important for every person who aspires to be a godly leader in their home, church, business, and community.

- God's Choice for Leadership: Broken Vessels, Strong Foundations

- The Heart of Leadership: Prayer, Faith, and Vision

- Leadership Hurdles: Clearing Them for the Long Haul
- The Scope of Leadership: A Mandate to Change the World

DNA Outreach Ministry

From Hell to Eternity outreach events feature Phil's testimony where he describes combat in his childhood and Viet Nam and how God used the experience of a friend dying in his place to provide a picture ten years later, showing that Jesus Christ had died for him, was resurrected, and lives today. He also recounts how he destroyed his marriage with Susy and how the Lord rebuilt it through His grace and forgiveness. Phil endeavors to clearly present the gospel with an invitation for those present to receive Jesus Christ as Lord and Savior.

Contact DNA

To discuss a conference, retreat, or church event, you can reach Phil Downer at 423.886.6362 or by e-mailing him at PhilDowner@DNAministries.org. For information about books, video or audio series, upcoming events in your area, references and endorsements, or the Downer family, check the DNA Ministries website at www.DNAministries.org.

APPENDIX E

A Note from David & Teresa

Our deepest desire is that through the sharing of our journey, others will come to deepen their relationship with God and strengthen their relationships in marriage, family, and the church. God has done a remarkable work of transformation in our own lives and it is now our joy to share what He has done with others.

From Teresa:

David and I have a particular passion for encouraging the marriages and families of ministry leaders. Getting married at sixteen and beginning a family by the age of seventeen (without the Lord in our lives!) allows you to know a great deal about the "wrong way" to do relationships. And even as we came to know Christ personally and lived out our calling to church ministry, we still struggled with how to love one another in a way that made a difference. But as David and I came to understand the "not good" of aloneness in our marriage and how we were created to meet God-given relational needs for one another—our marriage began to change. Please let us know if we can be of help to you and your marriage or family. Our *Galatians 6:6* ministry addresses the particular needs of ministry marriages and our *Center for Relational Care* provides help and enrichment for all relationships. Our *Training Workshops* can equip you in how to effectively minister to other individuals, marriages, and families. So please contact our office if we can be of further assistance: www.GreatCommandment.net or #800-881-8008 Ext. 219.

From David:

The Lord has done amazing things in my relationship with Teresa, our children, and now in the lives of our grandchildren. Our marriage was changed when we began to meet needs instead of point fingers. Our family was changed when we began to see the aloneness in the hearts of our children, and not just the ways that they needed to improve their behavior. Consequently, Teresa and I can testify to this: When we truly begin to experience His Word, relationships are different. Living out His simple commandment of loving God and His people, changes things!

Just as our marriage and family have changed, Teresa and I have seen entire church ministries and denominational movements transformed because of this simple truth of loving God and one another. When churches have begun to meet the relational needs of those without Christ, evangelism is revitalized. When church leaders have begun to see the aloneness in the hearts of their congregation, church ministry becomes relevant. When denominational leaders prioritize people over programs, ministry impact is re-energized.

Teresa and I believe it is our life's purpose to come alongside other ministries and ministry leaders, helping them to live out this Great Commandment message. Our ministry offers *Training Conferences, Ministry Consultations,* and *Coaching* all designed to equip others in Great Commandment ministry. So if we can be of support to you, your church, or even your denomination, we would love the chance to speak with you. Please contact our office and let us know how we might serve you and the Kingdom: www.GreatCommandment.net or #800-881-8008 Ext. 219.

APPENDIX F

About David & Teresa

D r. David and Teresa Ferguson have shared a biblical message of relational health and relevance for more than twenty-five years. Early in his church ministry, David, like so many in Christian ministries, tried unsuccessfully to achieve balance between ministry and family demands. Out of an intense desire to honor God and minister to the needs of his family, David rediscovered a biblical principle that transformed his life, his family, and his ministry to others. This gave birth to Ferguson's current passion: seeing the Great Commandment of loving God and loving others lived out among God's people. David and Teresa have now had the privilege to impact over 40,000 churches, ministers, and their laity.

As co-directors of the Great Commandment Network and Intimate Life Ministries, they direct a multi-disciplinary team who serves churches in the United States and abroad with training and resources through the strategic partners involved in the Great Commandment Network of denominations, movements, and ministries. David also serves as co-director of the Center for Relational Leadership who provides training and resources in church, business, and community settings. Teresa serves Intimate Life Ministries and the Center for Relational Leadership as a conference speaker, small group facilitator, and mentor for church and business leaders.

The Fergusons have written over a dozen books and other publications. They speak extensively at seminars, conferences, and workshops throughout the United States, the Virgin Islands, England, Ireland, Eastern Europe, and South Africa. They are the featured guests on the syndicated Intimate Life radio program and have appeared on COPE television programs, the Coral Ridge Hour, Family Life Today, and Parent Talk. David and Teresa also lecture at colleges and seminaries in the United States and abroad.

David and Teresa have been married for more than forty years. David has a M.Ed. from Southwest Texas State University and two doctoral degrees from Oxford Graduate School. He is a member of the Oxford Society of Scholars. They reside in Austin, Texas, and have three adult children – Terri, Robin and Eric – and six beautiful grandchildren.

APPENDIX G

The Great Commandment Network

The **Great Commandment Network** is a team of denominational partners, churches, para-church ministries, and strategic ministry leaders who are committed to the development of on-going Great Commandment ministries worldwide. Great Commandment ministries help us love God and our neighbors through deepening our intimacy with God and with others in marriage, family, church, and community relationships.

The Great Commandment Network is served by *Intimate Life Ministries* which includes:

• **The Center for Relational Leadership** – Their mission is to teach, train, and mentor both ministry and corporate leaders in Great Commandment principles, seeking to equip leaders with relational skills so they might lead as Jesus led. The CRL then challenges leaders to train their co-workers in these relevant, relational principles because great relational skills can and will impact customer/member satisfaction, morale, productivity, and ultimately, an organization's measurable success.

- **The Center for Relational Training** – Through a team of accredited community trainers, the CRT helps churches establish ongoing Great Commandment ministries. Experiential workshops are available in a variety of relational areas: Marriage, Parenting, Single Adult Relationships, Leadership, Emotional Fitness, Caregiving, and Spiritual Formation. These workshops are designed to support churches in their efforts to launch on-going relational ministries.

- **The Galatians 6:6 Retreat Ministry** – This ministry offers a unique two-day retreat for ministers and their spouses for personal renewal and for reestablishing and affirming ministry and family priorities. Co-sponsoring partners provide all meals and retreat accommodations as a gift to ministry leaders.

- **Great Commandment Radio** – Christian broadcasters, publishers, media, and other affiliates build cooperative relationships in order to see Great Commandment ministries multiplied.

- **Relationship Press** – This team collaborates, supports, and joins together with churches, denominational partners, and professional associates to develop, print, and produce resources that facilitate on-going Great Commandment ministry. Experiential, user-friendly curriculum materials allow individuals, churches, and entire denominations to deepen Great Commandment love.

The Great Commandment Network is also served by *The Center for Relational Care*:

- **The Center for Relational Care (CRC)** – Their mission is to equip churches to minister effectively to hurting people. The CRC provides therapy and support to relationships in crisis through an accelerated process of growth and healing, including Relational Care Intensives for couples, families, and singles. The CRC also offers training for counselors and caregivers through More Than Counseling seminars. www.RelationalCare.org

For more information on how you, your church, ministry, denomination, or movement can become part of the Great Commandment Network and take advantage of the services and resources offered by Intimate Life Ministries, write or call:

Intimate Life Ministries
P.O. Box 201808
Austin, TX 78720-1808
800-881-8008

Or visit our website:
www.GreatCommandment.net

The Great Commandment Network
and Intimate Life Ministries Provide the Following Resources and Training Opportunities

To assist churches, ministries, counselors, pastors and the local laity with the deepening of their love for God and one another, Intimate Life Ministries provides these, as well as many other opportunities for training and resources:

Resources

- **Intimate Encounters** *by Dr. David and Teresa Ferguson.* This 16 chapter resource focuses on subjects such as intimacy needs, childhood, and marital hurts, as well as goal setting in marriage. This workbook has been used by thousands of couples around the globe to enrich, strengthen, and heal marriages. Can be used in classes or small groups.

- **Intimate Encounters Leader's Kit** by Dr. *David and Teresa Ferguson.* The I.E. kit contains everything a leader needs to facilitate the *Intimate Encounters* material in a class or small group. DVDs and CDs show the authors presenting all 16 chapters of *Intimate Encounters* in 20-minute segments. The leader's kit contains a full leader's curriculum, reproducible masters, as well as two additional *Intimate Encounters* workbooks.

- **Top Ten Intimacy Needs** by *Ferguson and McMinn.* A great resource for ladies', men's, singles' or couples' small groups. Walks participants through each of the ten intimacy needs and how they are expressed in our relationship with God and with one another.

- **Emotional Fitness** by *Ferguson and McMinn.* Great for ladies', men's, singles' or couples' small groups. This resource identifies painful emotions that we all experience and then explains the biblical principles that can lead to healing and wholeness. Applies biblical antidotes that are applicable for every relationship.

- **Parenting with Intimacy** by *Ferguson, Warren, and Snead*. Learn how to love your children in the ways that God has uniquely designed just for them. Parents learn how to meet a child's relational needs, address a child's emotions according to biblical principles, and develop a close relationship that is foundational to the growth of every child.

- **Intimate Family Moments** by *Ferguson, Warren, and Snead*. With the use of Scripture, Bible dramas, discussion starters, and fun activities, families can experience biblical principles together. Contains lessons that are appropriate for preschool through high school.

- **Relational Foundations** by *Dr. David Ferguson*. This resource is designed to help believers recover a biblically-based relational mindset for life and ministry. It calls for a re-evaluation of some of the major elements of our faith and then asserts that all of these can only be properly understood within the context of loving relationships with God and one another.

- **Relational Discipleship** by *Dr. David Ferguson*. A fresh approach to spiritual formation which encourages believers to pursue the lifelong, life-changing, relational process of becoming like Jesus. This resource stresses that genuine discipleship grows out of a deep abiding relationship with the One who calls us to Himself.

Training

Intimate Life Ministries provides Relational Training Workshops in the following areas. These workshops are specifically designed to lead participants to experience biblical principles that are key to lasting change:

- **More Than Married Workshops** for married, engaged, and couples who are dating seriously

- **Parenting with Intimacy Workshops** for single parents, married parents, and childcare or educational providers

- **Discovering Intimacy Workshops** for single adults

- **Relational First Aid Workshops** for those who want to learn a biblical model for caregiving and ministry to others.

- **Emotional Fitness Workshops** for participants who want to learn the biblical principles that address each of our painful emotions and how to resolve them.

- **Servant Church Workshops** for churches and para-church ministries who want to increase the impact of their ministry as they learn how to deepen their love for God and strengthen their ability to show love for others.